# From Trafficking to Terror

A panic surrounds human trafficking and terrorism. The socially constructed "war on terror" and "war on trafficking" are inextricably linked through discourses that not only conflate the two, but help perpetuate anti-Muslim sentiments. Using ethnographic data and stories, *From Trafficking to Terror* juxtaposes lived experience with paradigms, policies, and rescue rhetoric, and presents the need to challenge the trafficking and terror paradigm and rethink approaches to the large scale challenges these discourses have created. This book is ideal for courses on gender, labor, migration, human rights, and globalization.

**Pardis Mahdavi**, PhD is associate professor of anthropology at Pomona College. Her research interests include gendered labor, migration, sexuality, human rights, youth culture, transnational feminism and public health in the context of changing global and political structures. Her first book, *Passionate Uprisings: Iran's Sexual Revolution*, was published with Stanford University Press in 2008, and her second book, *Gridlock: Labor, Migration and "Human Trafficking" in Dubai*, also Stanford University Press, is now available.

Pardis teaches courses on Medical Anthropology, Sociocultural Anthropology, Ethnographic Methods and has designed new courses entitled "Sexual Politics of the Middle East" and "Love, Labor and the Law." She has published in the *Journal of Middle East Women's Studies, Encyclopedia of Women in Islamic Cultures, Culture, Health and Sexuality, Social Identities, Comparative Studies of South Asia Africa and the Middle East, Anthropology News,* and the *Institute for the Study of Islam in the Modern World Review.* She has received fellowships and awards from institutions such as the American Council of Learned Societies, the Woodrow Wilson International Center for Scholars, the National Drug Research Institute, the American Public Health Association, and the Society for Applied Anthropology.

# Framing 21st Century Social Issues

The goal of this new, unique Series is to offer readable, teachable "thinking frames" on today's social problems and social issues by leading scholars. These are available for view on http://routledge.customgateway.com/routledge-social-issues.html.

For instructors teaching a wide range of courses in the social sciences, the Routledge *Social Issues Collection* now offers the best of both worlds: originally written short texts that provide "overviews" to important social issues *as well as* teachable excerpts from larger works previously published by Routledge and other presses.

As an instructor, click to the website to view the library and decide how to build your custom anthology and which thinking frames to assign. Students can choose to receive the assigned materials in print and/or electronic formats at an affordable price.

## Available

**Body Problems**
Running and Living Long in a Fast-Food Society
*Ben Agger*

**Sex, Drugs, and Death**
Addressing Youth Problems in American Society
*Tammy Anderson*

**The Stupidity Epidemic**
Worrying About Students, Schools, and America's Future
*Joel Best*

**Empire Versus Democracy**
The Triumph of Corporate and Military Power
*Carl Boggs*

**Contentious Identities**
Ethnic, Religious, and Nationalist Conflicts in Today's World
*Daniel Chirot*

**The Future of Higher Education**
*Dan Clawson and Max Page*

**Waste and Consumption**
Capitalism, the Environment, and the Life of Things
*Simonetta Falasca-Zamponi*

**Rapid Climate Change**
Causes, Consequences, and Solutions
*Scott G. McNall*

**The Problem of Emotions in Societies**
*Jonathan H. Turner*

**Outsourcing the Womb**
Race, Class, and Gestational Surrogacy in a Global Market
*France Winddance Twine*

**Changing Times for Black Professionals**
*Adia Harvey Wingfield*

**Why Nations Go to War**
A Sociology of Military Conflict
*Mark P. Worrell*

**How Ethical Systems Change**
Eugenics, the Final Solution, Bioethics
*Sheldon Ekland-Olson and Julie Beicken*

**How Ethical Systems Change**
Abortion and Neonatal Care
*Sheldon Ekland-Olson and Elyshian Aseltine*

**How Ethical Systems Change**
Tolerable Suffering and Assisted Dying
*Sheldon Ekland-Olson and Elyshian Aseltine*

**How Ethical Systems Change**
Lynching and Capital Punishment
*Sheldon Ekland-Olson and Danielle Dirks*

**Nuclear Family Values, Extended Family Lives**
*Natalia Sarkisian and Naomi Gerstel*

**Disposable Youth, Racialized Memories, and the Culture of Cruelty**
*Henry Giroux*

**Due Process Denied**
Detentions and Deportations in the United States
*Tany Golash-Boza*

**Oversharing**
Presentation of Self
in the Internet Age
*Ben Agger*

**Foreign Remedies**
What the Experience of Other Nations Can Tell Us about Next Steps in Reforming U.S. Health Care
*David A. Rochefort and Kevin P. Donnelly*

**DIY**
The Search for Control and
Self-Reliance in the 21st Century
*Kevin Wehr*

**Torture**
A Sociology of Violence and Human Rights
*Lisa Hajjar*

**Terror**
Social, Political, and Economic Perspectives
*Mark Worrell*

**Girls with Guns**
Firearms, Feminism, and Militarism
*France Winddance Twine*

**Beyond the Prison Industrial Complex**
Crime and Incarceration in the 21st Century
*Keven Wehr and Elyshia Aseltine*

**Unequal Prospects**
Is Working Longer the Answer
*Tay McNamara and John Williamson*

## Forthcoming

**The Pains of Mass Imprisonment**
*Benjamin Fleury-Steiner and Jamie G. Longazel*

**The Enduring Color Line in U.S. Athletics**
*Krystal Beamon*

**Identity Problems in the Facebook Era**
*Daniel Trottier*

# From Trafficking to Terror
## Constructing a Global Social Problem

Pardis Mahdavi

Pomona College

Routledge
Taylor & Francis Group

NEW YORK AND LONDON

First published 2014
by Routledge
711 Third Avenue, New York, NY 10017

and by Routledge
2 Park Square, Milton Park, Abingdon, Oxon OX14 4RN

*Routledge is an imprint of the Taylor & Francis Group, an informa business*

©2014 Taylor & Francis

The right of Pardis Mahdavi to be identified as author of this work has been asserted by her in accordance with sections 77 and 78 of the Copyright, Designs and Patents Act 1988.

**Trademark notice:** Product or corporate names may be trademarks or registered trademarks, and are used only for identification and explanation without intent to infringe.

*Library of Congress Cataloging in Publication Data*
Mahdavi, Pardis, 1978–
    From trafficking to terror : constructing a global social problem / Pardis Mahdavi, PhD. — 1 Edition.
    pages cm. — (Framing 21st century social issues)
    Includes bibliographical references and index.
    1. Human trafficking. 2. Forced labor. 3. Terrorism. I. Title.
    HQ281.M3244 2014
    306.3'62—dc23
    2013007414

ISBN13: 978-0-415-64212-5 (pbk)
ISBN13: 978-0-203-79537-8 (ebk)

Typeset in Garamond and Gill Sans
by EvS Communication Networx, Inc.

University Readers (www.universityreaders.com): Since 1992, University Readers has been a leading custom publishing service, providing reasonably priced, copyright-cleared, course packs, custom textbooks, and custom publishing services in print and digital formats to thousands of professors nationwide. The Routledge Custom Gateway provides easy access to thousands of readings from hundreds of books and articles via an online library. The partnership of University Readers and Routledge brings custom publishing expertise and deep academic content together to help professors create perfect course materials that is affordable for students.

Printed and bound in the United States of America by Publishers Graphics, LLC on sustainably sourced paper.

For Tara, my guiding star

# Contents

# Series Foreword

The early years of the 21st century have been a time of paradoxes. Growing prosperity and the growth of the middle classes in countries such as Brazil, China, India, Russia, and South Africa have been accompanied by climate change, environmental degradation, labor exploitation, gender inequalities, state censorship of social media, governmental corruption, and human rights abuses. Sociologists offer theories, concepts, and analytical frames that enable us to better understand the challenges and cultural transformations of the 21st century. How can we generate new forms of collective knowledge that can help solve some of our local, global, and transnational problems?

We live in a world in which new communication technologies and products such as cell phones, iPads, and new social media such as Facebook, Google, and Skype have transformed online education, global communication networks, local and transnational economies, facilitated revolutions such as the "Arab Spring," and generated new forms of entertainment, employment, protest, and pleasure. These social media have been utilized by social justice activists, political dissidents, educators, entrepreneurs, and multinational corporations. They have also been a source of corporate deviance and government corruption used as a form of surveillance that threatens democracy, privacy, creative expression, and political freedoms.

The goal of this series is to provide accessible and innovative analytical frames that examine a wide range of social issues including social media whose impact is local, global, and transnational. Sociologists are ideally poised to contribute to a global conversation about a range of issues such as the impact of mass incarceration on local economies, medical technologies, health disparities, violence, torture, transnational migration, militarism, and the AIDS epidemic.

The books in this series introduce a wide range of analytical frames that dissect and discuss social problems and social pleasures. These books also engage and intervene directly with current debates within the social sciences over how best to define, rethink, and respond to the social issues that characterize the early 21st century. The contributors to this series bring together the works of classical sociology into dialogue with contemporary social theorists from diverse theoretical traditions including but not limited to feminist, Marxist, and European social theory.

Readers do not need an extensive background in academic sociology to benefit from these books. Each book is student-friendly in that we provide glossaries of terms for the uninitiated that appear in bold in the text. Each chapter ends with questions for further thought and discussion. The books are the ideal level for undergraduates because they are accessible without sacrificing a theoretically sophisticated and innovative analysis.

This is the fourth year of our Routledge Social Issues Book series. Ben Agger was the former editor of this series during its first three years. These books explore contemporary social problems in ways that introduce basic sociological concepts in the social sciences, cover key literature in the field, and offer original diagnoses. Our series includes books on a broad range of topics including climate change, consumption, eugenics, torture, surrogacy, gun violence, the Internet, and youth culture.

This book by Pardis Mahdavi on the moral discourses that structure how the U.S. government defines, criminalizes, and interprets human trafficking is timely. Mahdavi provides an innovative analysis of how human trafficking cannot be understood without a careful analysis of the war on terror, which disempowers labor migrants, particularly women who work in the sex industry. Her analysis of the war on trafficking and the war on terror illuminates how the actual experiences of many migrants are neglected and distorted. This book also contributes a unique analysis of the role of corporations such as Google in public policy debates about human trafficking and human rights. This volume is ideal for courses on gender, globalization, immigration, sociology of law, and human rights.

France Winddance Twine
*Series Editor*

# Preface

This is a book about the production of panic about human trafficking, terrorism, Islamophobia, and the confluence of these anxieties. The production of panic about social issues, however, is not limited to any region or point in time. Therefore, the book deploys case studies from around the world and across time to examine ways in which the war on trafficking and the war on terror have become interconnected to the point of producing a large-scale moral panic about supposed victims and villains.

Drawing on fieldwork conducted in the United Arab Emirates (UAE) and in Washington D.C. between 2007 and 2011, this book examines the production and "othering" of Muslims and migrants (note that the categories are not mutually exclusive) through discourses and policies on trafficking and terror. This book is about Islamophobia, or a fabricated fear of Muslims, as it is sexualized, racialized, and gendered. Rather than bifurcate areas of inquiry such as discourse and policy, racialization and sexualization, or trafficking and terror, I focus on the conceptual linkages of the paradigms on trafficking and terror. I look, therefore, at two interrelated questions: (1) What are the consequences of the overlap between the wars on terror and trafficking? (2) How have these two wars furthered Islamophobia? Indeed, responses to the war on terror have been linked to policies designed to combat trafficking, and skills learned in one war are being deployed in the other—both in an attempt to securitize or control bodies, populations, and the "other."

Though each of these wars has been separately examined in detail over the past decade, the intersection of the two has gone largely unnoticed. Most pressing perhaps is the fact that the creations of stereotypes through these wars are among the most challenging social problems of our time. Undergraduate and graduate students alike will be able to consider how their experiences and the discourses they have been exposed to have contributed to the creation of problematic paradigms.

Fundamentally, the book looks at social justice issues that arise from the perpetuation of stereotypes in the form of policies and public portraitures. As an applied anthropologist, I aim to show how scholarly research can be used and applied beyond the classroom to impact social change. Throughout the book I draw on ethnographic research to show the glaring disconnects between policy and lived reality. I demonstrate how this type of research can be used to inform policy and affect social change. Students interested in social justice, human rights and applied scholarship will be able to connect with this approach.

*From Trafficking to Terror* is located at the confluence of anthropology, sociology, sexuality studies, public health, gender studies, ethnic studies, urban studies, and Middle Eastern studies. It is best suited to students in the social sciences writ large, though cultural studies students or those with an interest in area studies within the humanities may also find it useful and of interest. The central themes will be of importance for students in all levels of course work, and the presentation of the issues can be tailored to both undergraduates and graduates alike.

# Acknowledgments

The research for this book would not have been possible without the generous support of the American Council of Learned Societies, the Woodrow Wilson International Center for Scholars, and Google Ideas. Google Ideas, in particular, provided not only monetary support, but played a major role in facilitating the research. In addition, the infrastructural support of my wonderful employer, Pomona College, was crucial to the completion of the manuscript. Several research assistants helped me at various stages of the writing of this text including: Lila Glick, Justin Gutzwa, Abby Jordan, and Hannah Chasnov. I am grateful for the time and dedication they put into this project, most of them during their senior year. I could not have dreamed of a better editor to work with than Winddance Twine, who was not only my editor, but my mentor and the person who believed in the project from the beginning. I am grateful to Steve Rutter and the entire team at Routledge who worked tirelessly and seamlessly to make this book happen. Finally, I want to thank my incredible family, without whose support I could never even have begun work on this project. My parents, Mahmood and Fereshteh, and my brothers, Paymohn and Paasha, are always there for me when I need them. Most of all, I am grateful to my daughter, Tara, for giving me perspective, my incredible partner, Peter, for making it possible for me to think clearly when I could hardly form a sentence, and my son, Shayan, for being born exactly once the manuscript was completed.

# Prologue: Producing Panic, Pleading for Power

T his is a book about producing panic about human trafficking, terrorism, Islamophobia, and the confluence of these anxieties. The production of panic about social issues, however, is not limited to any region or point in time. On November 6, 2012, California residents voted on Proposition 35, entitled the Californians Against Sexual Exploitation Act (CASE). Proposition 35 was billed as a major counter-trafficking legislature and passed overwhelmingly with over nine million voters (or 81%) in favor. The language of the advertising in favor of Proposition 35 was clear: it was a moral duty to vote Yes on Proposition 35 in order to "fight human trafficking." After all, who could be opposed to fighting **trafficking**? If you were against Proposition 35, you must be for human trafficking. The decision was supposed to be clear-cut and simple. However, like many of today's political and pressing topics, the reality is much more complicated and reveals the clear undertones of a **moral panic**. According to Stanley Cohen, author of *Folk Devils and Moral Panics* (1972), a moral panic occurs when "[a] condition, episode, person or group of persons emerges to become defined as a threat to societal values and interests" (2). The language of moral panic typically harnesses a sense of moral indignation to create a category of villains or "folk devils" (Cohen 1972) which the public is to rally against.

If we examine the language in the official California state voter's guide, we find striking similarities between Proposition 35 and the larger international debates on the **war on terror** and the **war on trafficking**. According to the California official state voter guide, there were two case summaries defining the contours of what Proposition 35 promised. The short case summary defined the act as one that "increases prison sentences and fines for human trafficking convictions. Requires convicted human traffickers to register as sex offenders. Requires registered sex offenders to disclose Internet activities and identities." The longer case summary which was presented on some (but not all) ballots included the following:

1. Increases criminal penalties for human trafficking, including prison sentences up to 15-years-to-life and fines up to $1,500,000,
2. Fines collected to be used for victim services and law enforcement,
3. Requires person convicted of trafficking to register as sex offender,

4.  Requires sex offenders to provide information regarding Internet access and identities they use in online activities,
5.  Prohibits evidence that victim engaged in sexual conduct from being used against victim in court proceedings,
6.  Requires human trafficking training for police officers. (California General Election Official Voter Information Guide 2012)

Proposition 35 passed on election day. However, the day after the election, in response to a lawsuit filed by the American Civil Liberties Union (ACLU) on behalf of two anonymous sex offenders, a federal judge issued a restraining order that prevented the Act from going into effect. The restraining order is temporary, and at this time the trial is still pending.

What is most notable in this campaign is that Proposition 35 focused the entire issue of human trafficking on **sex trafficking**, and painted the problem as one that affects only women and children, and only in the sex industry. Those experiencing force, fraud, or coercion (the defining aspects of human trafficking as outlined by the United Nations **Palermo Protocol** to Prevent, Suppress and Punish Trafficking in Persons, Especially Women and Children 2000) who are outside the sex industry—laborers such as domestic workers, garment workers, or farm workers—or who are not women or children are rendered invisible by the language emphasized in Proposition 35. Furthermore, Proposition 35 is focused on criminalization and punishment as opposed to prevention. Over the years research by sociologists such as Elizabeth Bernstein has shown that a criminalization framework that focuses further on punishment does not help survivors of trafficking and only drives the source, supply, and demand for a particular economy or service further underground where it is more difficult to provide outreach. Moreover, survivors of trafficking and sex workers report that members of law enforcement are usually abusive during raids and arrests; Proposition 35 promised to give law enforcement *more* power to continue their abuse rather than put in a system of checks and balances.

There is a dramatic discrepancy between the amounts of funding behind each side. As of November 3, 2012, the campaign to promote Proposition 35 had raised over three million dollars while opponents to the Act had not raised even one dollar. Behind the question of funding stood the supporters and opponents, and it is important to take a closer to look to see the composition of persons in favor of and against the CASE Act. The most vocal supporters of Proposition 35 were members of church and religious organizations, several journalists and members of the media, and people such as Chris Kelley, an executive at Facebook, who contributed over two million dollars to the "Yes on Prop 35" campaign. The supporters were not people who would be directly affected by the passage of the legislature. By contrast, opponents of the CASE Act included laborers in the sex industry, members of organizations who do outreach to survivors of trafficking, and workers in other industries (such as agriculture) who experience forced labor daily.

The shortcomings of Proposition 35 are many, not the least of which is how the issue was presented, what it assumed, what it reinforced, and how it exemplified yet another disconnect between policy and the realities of lived experience. In addition to the focus on the sex industry as outlined above, the goal of the Proposition is to give more funding and power to law enforcement rather than promote decriminalization or an assessment of the larger structural issues that render populations vulnerable to force, fraud, or coercion such as poverty and the lack of housing or stable homes. Instead of promoting protection or the strengthening of social services such as the foster care system or the proliferation of shelters and outreach to vulnerable populations *before* they are coerced into labor, Proposition 35 focused on increased power and funding to law enforcement and harsher penalties and punishment for trafficking, both measures which have been proven ineffective by researchers on this issue. Finally, as many legal scholars[1] can attest, the language of Proposition 35 was deliberately ambiguous and dangerously sloppy. For instance, the pressure to punish any beneficiaries of the sex industry means that partners or children of consenting sex workers who benefit from their wages would be prosecuted as traffickers and clients must register as sex offenders for life. Indeed, the day after the passage of the act, the daughter of a sex worker from San Francisco with whom I had worked many years ago called me in tears. "Because my mom paid for my schooling, I will now be seen as a beneficiary of the sex industry. Now I can be prosecuted," she said. Other articles written before the campaign by opponents of Proposition 35 who were beneficiaries of the incomes of sex workers echoed this sentiment (Trafficking in Wrongs n.d.).

The coercion of some young women into the sex industry is cause for outrage. However, the language used in the ads, and the lack of actual data upon which the ads drew their reasoning was problematic. Advertisements featured extremely young, white women and girls who faced the camera to beg the viewer for help, thus reinforcing a rescue narrative (which scholars such as Gretchen Soduerland and others have challenged, noting that most survivors actually rescue themselves). The focus of the ads was on the fact that the women were (1) young, (2) innocent (as their narratives continuously emphasized), and (3) white. In one of the ads a woman named Sharmin Bock, who was billed as a "nationally recognized human trafficking prosecutor," emphatically noted: "right now as it stands if you are a child trafficked from China to California you have a greater protection under our federal laws than a child that gets trafficked from Fresno to Sacramento." That the women in question were American

---

1   See, for example, the writings of Garrity-Bond, Kim, or Haynes.

and white was of paramount importance to the construction of the campaign which was supposed to elicit *more* outrage. Another ad featured a politician asking the viewer, "We know it happens in other places, but how can we let this take place in California?" reinforcing an inherent **racialized morality** and ethnocentric point of view.

The language of Proposition 35 drew on and helped perpetuate a sense of moral panic in an attempt to bolster a **moral crusade** against the sex industry. These campaigns are referred to as moral crusades because the claims about the particular issues and the way they are framed are often infused with a sense of morality and are more damaging than the actual conditions. Like trafficking itself, this type of racialized moral panic is not new, nor is it unique to California or the United States. Sexual labor and **sex work** have always been moralized and racialized. In particular, the language of moral panic has long been deployed to elicit public outrage in a large-scale panic that would give power to some, further deny **agency** to vulnerable populations, and carve the world into victims and villains. Below, I delineate how moral panics and moral crusades are produced before moving to some historical and global examples and their racialized and moralizing reverberations.

## From Moral Panics to Moral Crusades

A close look at different types of hysteria around moral panic reveals a common theme of core components which include the proliferation of fear, usually about a "threat" that is deemed both imminent and deviant and threatens to unravel or destabilize the social order, ultimately leading to the creation of a stereotype with the help of narratives and imagery disseminated by the mass media. What is perhaps of most concern about moral panics is that they often result in large-scale witch hunts, such as those of the 17th century fueled by a war of religion, and during which an estimated 200,000 to 500,000 people were tortured and executed by burning, drowning, and hanging (Goode and Ben-Yehuda 1994: 178). The witch hunts of today, however, take the form of policy and legislative enactments that demonize a particular segment of society by highlighting a constructed (and often fabricated) problem with solutions that often are oppressive toward vulnerable populations but which must nevertheless be accepted due to new laws. The result of moral panics which contravene our human rights include the censoring of classic books and art, legislature creating oppressive statutes regarding peoples' private sexual practices, restrictions in adult entertainment, and over sensitivity to perfectly normal practices such as kissing your own children on the lips and taking photos of them at school. Also, there are those acts of moral panics which border on the ridiculous; for example, Tinky Winky the Teletubby and Dumbledore from Harry Potter being gay, which has resulted in the banning or censorship of these materials. By distorting statistics or omitting the whole truth, politicians can play to whatever emotion or sense of moral righteousness they want. It must be argued that the concept of moral panic is one of the most important factors in the public acceptance of normally unacceptable behavior.

It is of particular importance to underscore the socially constructed nature of moral panics. The social constructionist perspective highlights the fact that "social conditions become 'problems' only as a result of claims-making by interested parties, claims that may or may not reflect actual social arrangements" (Weitzer 2007: 448). In other words, that panics are socially constructed highlights the fact that the problems are not natural or existing problems, but are constructed by a group or multiple groups with particular agendas. This construction comes in the form of creating narratives or messaging campaigns such as those espoused by Proposition 35 or the war on terror, which are then perpetuated by the media. For example, going back to Proposition 35, the moral crusade around the act led the focus of human trafficking to be exclusively on the sex industry, and within the sex industry, created only young, white women as acceptable victims. This hysteria was damaging to all involved including the laborers outside the sex industry whose experiences were eclipsed, those in the sex industry who were *not* trafficked and who suddenly became subject to hyperscrutiny, and members of the families and friends of those in the sex industry who suddenly had to register as traffickers and sex offenders. Moreover, the way in which the narrative was constructed focused on young, white women who were kidnapped or taken, revealed a racialized morality. As scholars such as Goode and Ben-Yehuda (1994) have argued, moral panics lead to socially constructed notions of deviance which are often racialized.

Moral crusades, according to sociologist Ronald Weitzer, are "one of the forces responsible for transforming such conditions (of for example sex work) into 'problems.' These movements define a particular condition as an unqualified evil and see their mission as a righteous enterprise whose goals are both symbolic (attempting to redraw or bolster normative boundaries and moral standards) and instrumental (providing relief to victims, punishing evildoers)" (Weitzer 2007: 325). It is often the case that those leading the crusade are not actually members of the affected group, but rather activists with an agenda to foster public anxiety or panic and lobby policy makers to construct legislature that increases criminalization and punishment of particular groups to a certain end.

Some of the defining features of moral crusades which render them problematic include:

- exaggerating claims about the magnitude of the problem (often by relying on fabricated or unverified or verifiable statistics);
- a reliance on shock value or horror stories wherein the most extreme cases are highlighted as the norm and painted as occurring on a regular basis;
- using this shock value to justify harsh or draconian interventions as the only possible answer to safeguard the morality of the larger population;

- rhetoric which oversimplifies the problem, thereby rendering it unambiguous and indisputable.

All of these rely on the *social* production of a problem which becomes part of an agenda to vilify certain groups and ensure that particular legislature (such as Proposition 35) is passed. While many scholars have looked at the ways in which moral panics structure and produce or construct deviance (Goode and Ben-Yehuda 1994; Weitzer 2007), increased attention is needed to the impact of moral panics on public perceptions of deviance and social problems.

## Moral Panics Across Time and Space

Moral panics and moral crusades are not limited to California or to any specific region. In fact, we can see both historical and global instances of where particular issues have become cause for moral panic and resultant legislation. An assessment of the historical and global reach of moral panics is useful to see the magnitude and reverberations of these socially constructed panics. What is also of note when looking across time and cultures are the particular issues and populations that do *and* do not trigger moral panics. A look at issues that do raise public indignation reveals the racialized nature of issues such as sexuality, sex work, migration, and human trafficking.

It is important to underscore the fact that moral panics do not focus exclusively on race, class, gender, or sexuality, but often draw upon at least a few of these intersecting categories. Within the United States we have seen historical examples of moral panics focusing on issues such as drug use including but not limited to: (1) reefer madness and the consequences of marijuana use; (2) panics about crack moms and crack babies, which caused addicted pregnant women to be seen and treated as criminals, and which over simplified media coverage leading to harsh social agendas regarding women and minorities; and (3) the war on drugs, initiated by President Nixon in 1971 to discourage the production, distribution, and consumption of illegal psychoactive drugs, and which labeled drug abuse as the most important problem facing the country at the time (Goode and Ben-Yehuda 1994: 63). All three of these panics include anxiety over racialized bodies need to be monitored or disciplined. In the case of all three of these examples, moral panics led to the issuance of legislature that further criminalized already marginalized populations. The after effects of moral panics around crack moms and the war on drugs can be felt today in the high incarceration and forced sterilization rates of certain racialized populations. Other examples of moral panics in the United States include anxieties about the Red Scare or threat of communism in the forties and fifties, and the more recent panic about whether or not certain computer games (such as Dungeons and Dragons) encourage paganism.

## The White Slavery Panic

While not all moral panics focus on issues pertaining to sexuality or trafficking, there are a few prominent historical and global examples that do. Moreover, the issues that do elicit moral panic regarding sexuality underscore the racialized undertones inherent in panics about human trafficking, migration, and labor while others go unnoticed. Panics around human trafficking that focus the issue on the sex industry have historical origins dating back at least as far as the panic over the white slave trade, which began in the late 19th and early 20th centuries in both Europe and the United States.

The white slavery panics were a series of moral panics wherein fantastical tales of women who were young, white, and usually of European or American descent were kidnapped and sold into sexual slavery. Some scholars point to a series of journalistic pieces published in the United Kingdom as the start of the panic (Doezema 2005; Walkowitz 1992). These stories, sensationally titled the "Maiden Tribute of Babylon" focused on tales of young, innocent, white, virgins who were being lured into erotic encounters with older males (Walkowitz 1992; Vance and Miller 2004). These pieces functioned to accomplish several goals. First, the moral panic around the white slave trade linked prostitution to slavery in the minds of the public. From here on, prostitution and slavery, as well as migration and prostitution, would be forever linked through this far reaching moral panic. Scholars have traced the history of the white slave trade and the contemporary manifestations of the moral panic around prostitution, sex trafficking, migration, and human trafficking (Doezema 2005; Vance and Miller 2004; Walkowitz 1992; Wijers 1998). What is important to underscore here is the rampant racialized morality that focused this panic. While the stories about white slavery began with upper-class men in London, the stories grew "more fantastical over time until news papers were reporting on alleged cases in which 'respectable women' were abducted and sold into slavery in the Ottoman harem" (http://www.wisegeek. com/what-is-white-slavery.htm). This was the beginning of the creation of "folk devils" (Cohen 1972) or villains who were seen as the "other."

The moral panic around the white slave trade quickly spread to the United States and took root in the years leading up to World War I. Rather than focusing on the Ottomans or other Middle Eastern villains, the moral panic in the United States instead pointed to Chinese immigrants, who were narrated as having created large rings of white sex slaves that were servicing immigrants and others alike. Like other moral panics, the media led the structuring of the narrative with the Pulitzer and Hearst papers among the major participants who spread anti-immigrant sentiment while perpetuating a panic about young, white women being forced into prostitution. As in Proposition 35 and many other moral panics, this fervor resulted in the passage in 1910 of the **Mann Act**, which specifically outlawed enticing women across state borders for the purpose of prostitution. What is perhaps most interesting about the moral panic about white slavery is that there is little data or evidence to demonstrate whether or not there was any thing whatsoever to base this large-scale movement upon.

The moral panic around white slavery reveals the many pitfalls of the current moral panic around human trafficking and sex work that structured the passage of Proposition 35. First, the supposed victims were all cast as innocent, young, white women, and the slavery was supposedly made more horrific by the fact that it involved women of European descent. Around the same time as the panic over white slavery arose, there were hundreds if not thousands of women from different parts of Asia working in the sex industry, sometimes by choice, but often against their will, within military camps and in the United States. These women, sometimes referred to as "comfort women," did not elicit the same type of moral panic ostensibly because of the racialized background of the women. Narratives and uproar around the white slave trade reflected cultural attitudes about people of other races, including beliefs that people of other racial origins didn't view being enslaved in the same way that Europeans did. Furthermore, white slavery panics also played on racial panics, reinforcing racial divides and contributing to hostile attitudes about people of other races through the creation of particular victims and villains. This certainly served a political goal; in the United States, for example, anti-Chinese sentiment allowed discriminatory laws to persist well into the 20th century.

Beyond the false linkages created in the minds of the public between prostitution, race, migration, and slavery, the white slavery panics ignored the very real issues of forced labor and servitude that were actually occurring at the turn of the 20th century. Children, for example, were forced to work in factories in both the United States and Britain, while sharecroppers in regions like the American South were experiencing high levels of abuse and made to work long hours without pay (not unlike migrant domestic and agricultural workers to this day).

A look at moral panics across both time and space reveals the many linkages in the ways in which narratives are deployed to vilify particular populations. In the panic over the white slave trade, and later in the war on terror, war on trafficking, and even Proposition 35, we can see ways in which certain populations are cast as in need of saving while others are painted as villains in need of monitoring or **surveillance**. The racialized nature of these panics persists to this day as a new type of moral panic is emerging in the United States. This new moral panic sutures sex work, human trafficking, terrorism, and migration in an attempt to promote fear mongering while fingering Muslims (possible terrorists) as those in need of monitoring. By wedding panic over human trafficking to the panic about terrorism, a new, powerful enemy emerges, while we see a renewed energy to protect particular victims from these newly created villains. The result is a series of subversive policies and rhetoric that, like the moral panics that serve as the precursors, have the potential to do significant damage and further racial divides.

### *Looking Ahead*

That there have been moral panics about trafficking is not new. Nor is the fact that there have been panics about immigration or sex work. But what I'm introducing in this text is a new, more subversive type of moral panic, one which sutures panic about immigration, sexuality, sex work, trafficking, and terrorism all into one. Because it draws on many narratives, this has the potential to be the most damaging and destructive moral panic of our time.

For this reason, it is important to explore the linkages created in the minds of the public between terrorism, trafficking, gender, sexuality, and a dreaded fear of Muslim populations which is leading to worldwide inequality and injustice today.

# 1: Trafficking Terror and Terrorizing Trafficking

<hr style="width:15%"/>

"*Why is Iran on Tier 3 of the Trafficking in Persons Report (TIP)?*" *I ask the group of state department officials gathered in the conference room of the U.S. Office to Monitor and Combat Trafficking in Persons. Silence descends on the room as the question hangs in the air. I repeat my question, hoping that one among the five top level officials who have been appointed to combat trafficking have an answer that explains why a particular country has received the lowest possible ranking in the TIP report, a global scorecard ranking 180 countries around the world based on an opaque system set up to respond to the war on trafficking. I have long been frustrated at the mercurial compilation of the reports that make presumptions and draw on under-researched evidence—sometimes rumors even—to paint a picture of what trafficking is about.*

*"I think, I think maybe it's because of their involvement in terrorism," one official finally answers, looking around the room at his colleagues. "That, and it's probably easier to leave them there given their track record on other things like terror and such," adds the woman sitting to his right.*

*"But what do those have to do with trafficking?" I press further. "How is it that a country could receive the lowest ranking in the TIP, be subjected to sanctions based on this ranking, and the reasons behind it remain opaque?"*

*"You are probably right in that we should re-think our Iran stance, but we know that it's all part and parcel of the same thing, trafficking and terror, and those countries, they are notorious for being involved in both," the official sitting to my right answers, scribbling notes furiously on his pad while his colleagues stand up as if to indicate that the meeting is over. I have obviously touched a nerve, and my accusations that the war on trafficking has been drawing on and perpetuating anti-Muslim sentiment have not been—unsurprisingly—well received. I am ushered into the corridor, handed a card, and thanked for my time. "We will be in touch, you raise some good questions, but there is only so much we can do," the woman tells me as she pushes the elevator button to ensure that I am on my way out* (Fieldnotes, Washington, D.C., September 1, 2009).

## Introduction: The Terror of Trafficking

Some of today's most troubling moral crusades feature race, class, gender, and sexuality colliding in public conversations about both terrorism and trafficking. Prior to the controversy around Proposition 35, moral panics around sex work, human trafficking and the dreaded "other" were bubbling up in the convergence of the wars on terror and trafficking. The year 2011 marks the tenth anniversary not only of the September 11th attacks on the World Trade Center—arguably resulting in the beginning of the U.S. war on terror—but it is also the tenth anniversary of the U.S. **Trafficking in Persons Report** (TIP n.d.), demarcating the beginning (or what some might call resurgence) of the global war on "trafficking."[1]

A decade into two of America's most damaging and elusive wars presents a good time for reflection about the reverberations and global ramifications of U.S. foreign policy which has been informed by a larger moral crusade. The war on terror and the war on trafficking, two seemingly separate initiatives, have become interwoven in recent years and conspire to castigate Muslim majority countries as sites of depravity, difference, and danger, fueling racist rhetoric about the "clash of civilizations" (Huntington 1996). Both issues are influenced by notions of race, class, and gender, seeking to produce distinct stereotypes of victims and villains while the intersection of these two wars presents a convergence of moral panics, or public anxieties pertaining to immoral behavior about sexuality, Islam, and immigration. Each war seeks to marshal rhetoric about the other to further bolster its cause, and to justify the creation of harsh policies with overt condescension as well as interventions that currently are more harmful than the problems they seek to solve.

Though each of these wars has been separately examined in detail over the past decade, the intersection of the two has largely gone unnoticed. In this book, I draw on the lived realities of those affected by both terrorism and trafficking to challenge popular understandings of the scope of the problem. I look at ways in which conversations and thoughts about issues such as trafficking and terrorism have led to policies that not only are disconnected from lived realities on the ground, but are actually *increasing* challenges and human rights violations. Drawing on an analysis of films such as *Taken* and the recent writings and popularity of author and activists Nicholas Kristof and his wife Sheryl WuDunn, I examine the slippages between the two wars and demonstrate how they have become interconnected in many ways. The analysis is foregrounded in a combination of ethnography, discourse analysis, and policy review.

Between 2007 and 2010, I conducted ethnographic field research in the United Arab Emirates (UAE), working with survivors of trafficking as well as policy makers and those seeking to provide services to migrants. In 2009 and 2010, I spent eight months in Washington, D.C. where I interviewed U.S. government officials

---

1 I place these terms in quotes to indicate their contested nature and social construction within current paradigms of U.S. Empire. It is important to note that the panic over trafficking is not new to the 21st century but has roots that date back to panic over the white slave trade in the 18th century. For more historical context please see the work of Judith Walkowitz or Elizabeth Bernstein.

about their various positions on trafficking and terrorism. Finally, in 2012 I spent six months as a fellow at **Google Ideas**, a think tank branch of Google, where I helped to organize a large-scale initiative and summit on "Illicit Networks." This project brought me into contact with various stakeholders in the wars on terror and trafficking including government officials, high-level technology personnel, activists, and funders. In addition to a wide range of qualitative research that I conducted, this book also includes an analysis of policies and discourses that circulate in the United States and internationally.

When it comes to the wars on trafficking and terror, stereotypes and public controversy inform policies and vice versa. Unfortunately, both public representations and policy are damaging Muslim populations by perpetuating anti-Muslim sentiments and stereotypes. Furthermore, these same policies and representations are harmful to migrants, laborers, and trafficked persons of all religious and ethnic backgrounds.

The hyperscrutiny on sexuality within both the wars on terror and trafficking is resulting in the monitoring or **surveillance of sexuality**, calling for a militarization or securitization of sexuality. These public–political linkages are creating a legally produced criminality wherein laws and policies that are enacted to mitigate abuses of human rights are instead *exacerbating* the problem, leading more people into potentially abusive situations. Through a close examination of the production of public controversy and the wars on terror and trafficking, I will detail examples of the legal production of illegality as well as the negative effects of stereotypes, media hype, and policies pertaining to the wars on terror and trafficking.

## Defining the Problem—Producing the Wars on Terror and Trafficking

Throughout this book I will draw on a series of concepts, debates, and policy recommendations. It is useful to give broad definitions of some of these concepts, debates, and policy documents in order to provide the context that frames much of the ethnographic data presented by the stories and lived experiences of those most affected by the wars on trafficking and terror. Some of the concepts have fueled the production of artificial dichotomies and labels, so I will not only lay out the conceptual framework, but also present a brief analysis of those dichotomies at the outset.

The concept of agency is used throughout the text to refer to an individual's capacity, desire, and potential to make choices and decisions about his or her own life, trajectory, and future. Agency is the ability to act as an individual and to determine one's own fate. It is often thought to be limited by the concept of structure—the term used to refer to institutions or conditions that might restrict agency.[2] These structures

---

2  Some scholars have argued, and I agree, that it is not useful to dichotomize structure and agency, but rather to note that they may be on a continuum; that is, structures can limit or enable choices made to exert agency. For an in-depth discussion of this point please see the work of Nicole Constable, Philippe Bourgois, or Mitch Dunier.

or institutions can include systems such as education, employment sector, and state regulations, or socially constructed categories such as class, race, gender, ethnicity, nationality, or group identity. Individuals often find agency within the structures that seek to limit them, and exercise their agency in defiance of structures such as race, class, or gender.

Examining lived experience helps to show how people across the globe find pockets of resistance and agency in what may seem like contexts of terror and repression—structures that present significant challenges to migrants' agency as well as to their ideas about agency. The concept of agency is employed and highlighted to move beyond the traditional concept of Muslims and migrants (not that these categories are mutually exclusive) as victims solely of their own circumstances or as no more than terrorists and traffickers; this application of the concept of agency recognizes the choices made and the strategies employed by transnational migrants as enterprising and courageous persons seeking to make a better life for themselves and their families. Rather than describing something happening *to* migrants, the concept of agency is instrumental in delineating the deliberate choices migrants make to move into one industry or another, or to leave their home country in search of work. This concept will also come into play when interrogating the false (but accepted) dichotomy of force and choice within migration, trafficking, and terror.

The concept of agency is also particularly relevant to talking about and understanding the nature of sex work, which forms the basis of much of the trafficking debate. The reason I use the term "sex work" is to recognize the agency of persons involved in this industry, specifically those who view sex work as labor. In defining sex work, the United Nations definition embedded in the language of the report from the division of advancement for women recognizes sex work as a choice to engage in a specific type of labor and does not stigmatize the type of activities involved:

> The term, "sex work" or "commercial sex work" is generally understood to include a wide range of behaviors and venues, and includes, but is not limited to, street prostitution, brothel prostitution, exotic dancing, paid domination, and sexual massage. Many people who engage in sex work or commercial sex identify what they do as sex work, but it is also important to acknowledge that many other people who engage in informal and occasional sexual transactions may not incorporate this experience an important part of their personal identity.
>
> (U.S. Trafficking in Persons Report n.d.)

Thus the use of the term "sex work" is an attempt to situate the industry within a framework of labor so that those involved in the sex work industry can access the rights and protections afforded to other laborers. It is also an attempt to provide more agency for those involved in the industry, recognizing that not all persons engaging in sex work are victims or have been tricked or trafficked into this type of work.

A close examination of the nexus of trafficking and terror relies heavily on the concept of **discourse**. Discourse refers to the production of conversations, ideas, language and the way of discussing a subject that becomes regularized or institutionalized through repeated use.[3] When people use the term they are often referring to socially agreed upon or mainstream imaginings of an issue—the *constructed* nature of discourse must be underscored. By default, because discourse is defined as the majority viewpoint, other views that may not fit within the dominant version of the conversation may be excluded. Discourses can become paradigms, reflective of a certain moment that defines the mainstream. The concept is particularly useful in that it reminds us that dominant versions (or discourses) about an issue are always constructed. In the following pages, I use the concept of discourse to refer to the dominant paradigms about human trafficking, terrorism, Islamophobia, and labor migration, particularly as they pertain to and affect the wars on terror and trafficking.

I also look at how this discourse has been produced and circulates through mainstream media, journalistic representation of the issues, and policy and political documentations. Through this multilevel approach, I examine the effect of mainstream discourse on constructing policies about trafficking and terror, and point to ways in which both the discourse, and its ensuing policies, are not only different from the actual experiences and trajectories of migrants and/or trafficked persons, but also have impacted them negatively and exacerbated the situation of migrants and forced laborers in need.

Like the moral crusades described in the prologue, discourses on trafficking and terror, infused with morality, have been socially constructed to *create* ideas about deviance. Discourses are powerful because they influence and structure interventions and policies that may be disconnected from the realities of lived experience. In the case of both the wars on terror and trafficking, discourse and policy continue to reinforce one another, solidifying the idea that talk is not just talk, but can lead to interventions in the name of help, protection, or security. Discourse and policies regarding both the war on terror and the war on trafficking fuel and reproduce themselves, with policy slippages between the two wars.

The concept of discourse is particularly relevant when looking at the ways in which conversations, policies, and portrayals of trafficking align or disconnect with the definition of human trafficking (as outlined by The United Nations) and/or narratives of persons who have been labeled trafficked. The official definition of trafficking as stated in Article 3, paragraph (a) of the Protocol to Prevent, Suppress and Punish Trafficking in Persons prepared by the United Nations Office of Drug Control (note the disjuncture in the UN agency designated to monitor human trafficking—an agency

---

3  For a more in-depth discussion of the social construction of discourse, see Foucault 1972.

dedicated to organized crime and the movement of drugs rather than the human rights arm of the UN) is as follows:

> the recruitment, transportation, transfer, harbouring or receipt of persons, by means of the threat or use of force or other forms of coercion, of abduction, of fraud, of deception, of the abuse of power or of a position of vulnerability or of the giving or receiving of payments or benefits to achieve the consent of a person having control over another person, for the purpose of exploitation. Exploitation shall include, at a minimum, the exploitation of the prostitution of others or other forms of sexual exploitation, forced labour or services, slavery or practices similar to slavery, servitude or the removal of organs.

That this policy has been constructed within a framework of criminalization (rather than a framework of rights) is one aspect of the problem. Trafficking, and the rights of persons who have faced abuse within forced labor or migration, is a human rights issue, but has fallen under the umbrella of crime.

On the basis of the definition of trafficking given in this protocol, it is evident that trafficking in persons has three constituent elements: (1) *the act* (what is done; namely recruitment, transportation, transfer, harboring, or receipt of persons); (2) *the means* (how it is done, including the threat or use of force, coercion, abduction, fraud, deception, abuse of power or vulnerability, or giving payments or benefits to a person in control of the victim); and (3) *the purpose* (why it is done; possible categories here are for the purpose of exploitation, which includes exploiting the prostitution of others, sexual exploitation, forced labor, slavery or similar practices and the removal of organs).

While this is the definition used by the international community, the Palermo Protocol (2000) has a passage built into it that makes the state the ultimate investigator and enforcer of these crimes:

> To ascertain whether a particular circumstance constitutes trafficking in persons, consider the definition of trafficking in the Trafficking in Persons Protocol and the constituent elements of the offense, as defined by relevant domestic legislation.

While this is the agreed upon definition of trafficking in the international community, and this definition is broad enough to encapsulate a variety of abuses to migrants in a variety of sectors, the functional definition of the term—as produced and perpetuated by the discourse—has focused the issue on sex work. Moreover, each state has subtle nuances in the definition of trafficking, and more prominently, in deciding who counts as a trafficked person. This is perhaps best exemplified in a close reading of the United States' domestic and international policies on trafficking (which will be discussed later in the chapter) as they have played a major role in structuring the discourse on trafficking, and can also be read as products of discourse and debates about trafficking, migration, and sex work.

The war on terror is a phrase first used by George W. Bush to denote a military, legal, and ideological struggle against regimes and organizations that were labeled as "terrorists." More conceptually, the war on terror is about separating "good Muslims" from "bad Muslims" (Mamdani 2002), and producing a category of "terrifying Muslims" (Rana 2011) requiring intense surveillance at best and more often harsh responses such as intervention and detention. Used to justify intervention and military occupation of countries such as Afghanistan and Iraq, the term has also become emblematic of a witch hunt of sorts wherein it is not clear when or how this war could or would be won, and when or how it would end. Perhaps among the more damaging effects of this military and discursive war has been the portraiture of Muslims as dangerous or potential members of terrorist organizations and regimes. This has led to an atmosphere of *Islamophobia* or fear of Islam, as an ideology and way of life, which can restrict the agency of the individuals about whom these stereotypes have been constructed.

The war on trafficking focuses on women—what some might call "hyperfeminizing"—which stands in distinct opposition to the focus on policing men within the war on terror—a hypermasculinization. The widespread panic about transnational female labor, especially in the commercial sex industry, has resulted in an elasticity of the term "human trafficking" specifically as it is deployed in policy and international conventions. As scholars such as Nicole Constable (2010) and Julia O'Connell Davidson (2006) have noted, it is a term that claims too much and too little. Like a rubber band, the term "trafficking" stretches wide enough to encompass all forms of commercial sex work (whether forced, frauded, coerced, or not), but then shrinks to exclude forced labor outside the sex industry. The misunderstanding that human trafficking refers only to women who are kidnapped by men and forced into the sex industry has, problematically, become the functional definition of the term in policy, media and discourse. This hyperfeminized and hypersexualized term has altered the way in which trafficking is represented, pursued, and prosecuted. The paradigm of human trafficking as it exists today, and critically, the disjuncture between the legal ambiguity and popular specificity with which trafficking has been defined, offer uncomfortable insight into the complex ways that sexuality, gender, and race permeate popular understandings of victimhood, vulnerability, and power. Most notably, the trafficking discourse calls for policies to regulate or "securitize" sexuality.

The TIP report, up until 2009, was almost exclusively focused on a country's efforts to combat trafficking by focusing on sex trafficking. There was very little mention, if any, of forced labor and other issues faced by migrants outside the sex industry, an oversight that has led to a sexualization of the issue. The report, fueled by and helping propel larger discourses on Islamophobia and sexuality, prescribes country level recommendations; if these recommendations are not followed, countries are placed on a watch list, subject to non-humanitarian sanctions, and publicly castigated in the international community. The war on terror response is more extreme and results in full-scale invasion of a country where individual or groups of terrorists are thought to reside. Neither the war on terror nor the war on trafficking recognizes that the larger macro scope of the problem is rooted in rising inequality and a new economic world order where, in the case of trafficking, people must move across borders to make ends meet and are subsequently more susceptible to abuse. Both discourses also rely on the production of rhetoric about attacks on freedom, although the very framing of these discourses and policies attacks a very basic freedom, the freedom of movement.

Concerns about both Islam and immigration connect moral panics with the threat of "Islamic peril" and fears about migration in general. While the war on trafficking turns female migrants into victims without agency, the war on terror turns Muslim male migrants into villains—both categories inspiring panic, fear, and distrust. Discourses of the war on terror and Islamic peril perpetuates fear through threats of "sleeper cells connected by illicit transactions of money, goods and people across borders" (Rana 2011: 69), which can be seen in popular films such as *Syriana* or the television hit show *Sleeper Cells*. Equally problematic is the gendering of Muslim men in the war on terror as at once hypermasculinized in their capacity to destruct and oppress women, and also feminized and emasculated as can be seen in the case of Abu Ghraib.[4] These stereotypes have been developing in different paths but also often collide to reinforce images, discourse, and policy.

## Colliding Wars—Race and Sexuality

The war on terror and the war on trafficking share numerous commonalities, which construct the foundation for discourses that rely on a slippage between the two, connecting them and making them inextricably intertwined resulting in a new paradigm that carves the world into good guys and bad guys, who are deemed a threat to women everywhere. Both rely on images of dark skinned men often with Middle Eastern accents as bad guys (for a pop culture example of this consider films such as *Taken, Call and Response,* and *Human Trafficking*). The slippage of terror and trafficking results in policies further castigating Muslim men as the source of the problem while painting women in Muslim majority countries as lacking in agency and distinctively unmodern. In fact, as many scholars have noted (Abu Lughod 2002; Mahmood 2004; Spivak 2006), the figure of the Muslim or brown-skinned woman who needs to be saved from brown/Muslim men by white men was a central tenet of the discourse to

---

4   For a more detailed discussion of the gendering of Muslim men through the war on terror, see the excellent work of Jasbir Puar.

promote the war on terror and the eventual invasion of Afghanistan. The conceptual framings of "fighting terrorism" and "saving the poor oppressed women in burqa's" were connected in U.S. discourse to construct the trope or stereotype of the villainous Muslim man who needed to be attacked/punished/detained. Both the wars on terror and trafficking ascribe the source of the problem to individuals or rings of crime, trafficking, and terror, but both respond with policies or violence aimed at an entire country.

The confluence of race and sexuality in trafficking and terror can perhaps best be seen in three examples from mainstream media: (1) the anti-trafficking campaign Stop Child Sex Trafficking Now, supported by celebrities and bolstered by Facebook and Twitter, (2) the blockbuster success of the film *Taken,* and (3) the writings and activism of Nicholas Kristof and his wife, Sheryl WuDunn. Together, these examples have significantly shaped popular understandings of human trafficking and the Muslim world while drawing on rhetoric about the war on terror to fight the war on trafficking. These discourse makers also contribute to **tropes** about Muslim women and the need to save or protect these women through any means necessary, thus legitimating acts of violence across the world.

The intertwining of the wars on terror and trafficking can be disturbingly observed in the fact that responses to the war on trafficking are tied to the skills built in the war on terror. A recent anti-trafficking initiative sponsored by Asthon Kutcher, Microsoft, and Facebook is called Stop Child Sex Trafficking Now (SCTNow). The organization raises funds to "end demand" for sex, and to do so they have "partnered with specially trained operatives familiar with what it takes to infiltrate, investigate and bring justice to the predators victimizing children worldwide" (SCTNow n.d.). These operatives are those who were trained in the war on terror (and this selling point is made explicit on the organization's website and in their fundraising campaigns) and who "possess skills that enable them to achieve their goals in foreign lands independently, without support of U.S. law enforcement" (SCTNow n.d.). The organization promotes hiring these operatives because they can operate outside the law and infiltrate specific countries where the villains are thought to reside. Though these operatives have no experience or training in working with survivors of trafficking, they are being funded to cross borders (possibly violating state sovereignty) and take matters into their own hands.

A Hollywood example of the SCTNow campaign can be seen in the film *Taken.* Released in 2008, *Taken* is about an ex-CIA agent. played by Liam Neeson, whose daughter (a 15-year-old virgin) is kidnapped by dark-skinned traffickers with Middle Eastern accents while she is on vacation in Paris. As the film unfolds, the father chases his daughter across the globe, drawing on his counter-terrorism skills to murder and torture all who stand in his way with whatever means necessary; of note is the fact that he is never held accountable for this violence nor for violating state laws or sovereignty. It bears mentioning that this film was shot and released simultaneously with the George W. Bush White House attempting to justify torture and violence in Abu Ghraib, Iraq, and Afghanistan. At the end of the film, the father tracks his daughter to the yacht of a wealthy Arab sheikh (whom he promptly kills) just as she is about to be bought or traded. He rescues his daughter and returns home, not having to face any consequences for the violence inflicted throughout the movie. The message is clear: killing is justified if you are killing irrefutable bad guys.

As unsettling, racist, and Islamophobic as this plot line is, perhaps even more disturbing is the fact that the Liam Neeson character in the film was allegedly modeled after a retired Army Green Beret colonel named William Hillar. Hillar began touring the country, talking about his daughter who had been kidnapped while on vacation in Thailand. According to Hillar, however, the film deviates slightly from his life in that he was not able to save his daughter who was eventually killed. He marketed himself as a counter-terrorism expert who had come into contact with "the scum" who profit from illicit networks when his daughter was forced into sex trafficking. After the release of the movie, Hillar was in high demand, speaking at conventions across the country and actively fashioning himself as a leader in both the wars on terror and trafficking; audiences across the country received him as a hero. For a short period of time. In March of 2011 he was arrested and charged with several counts of fraud and mis-representation. Not only was he not a Green Beret and had never fought in any kind of war, but he never even had a daughter. It seems that *Taken*, as sex worker rights activist Emi Koyama has articulated "and it's simulacrum that is Bill Hillar—or was it the other way around? Is becoming part of the reality in the landscape of the anti-trafficking movement" (Koyama 2011: 27).

Hillar was one of the heroes of the movement and organization Stop Child Sex Trafficking Now, which builds on the *Taken* model to deploy skills learned in the war on terror to stop the war on trafficking. SCTNow describes its approach to trafficking:

> SCTNow has chosen to fund a bold, new approach, one that addresses the demand side of child sex trafficking by targeting buyers/predators for prosecution and conviction ... SCTNow has launched a national campaign to raise money for retired elite military operatives targeting demand side of trafficking ... These operatives use skills developed in the war on terror in this war to bring down predators. ... These teams possess skills beyond the average military or law enforcement, individual skills that enable them to achieve their goals in foreign lands independently, without support of U.S. law enforcement resources.
>
> (SCTNow n.d.)

Several things are worth noting within this approach. The first is the trope about ending demand that colors much anti-trafficking activism. What demand will be ended is unclear. Demand for intimacy? Love? Care? Or tourism? In addition, how this demand will be ended or the strategies employed to do so also remain opaque.

One is left to surmise that these special operatives will end demand by literally ending the lives of the predators. Also in question is the livelihood of women in the sex industry who will need to seek a new means of making ends meet if demand for their services is ended. (Bernstein 2007). Beyond the end demand confusion is the issue of relying on those experts who developed "special skills" in the war on terror. As Koyama notes, "these same 'experts led us to invade a country that had nothing to do with 9/11, detained Arab and Muslim Americans without due process, tortured innocent people as well as prisoners of war, conducted surveillance on Arab and Muslim communities in the U.S., 'renditioned' suspects to countries to outsource torture, and illegally wiretapped our telephone calls" (Koyama 2011: 28). While these operatives are celebrated for violating state sovereignty in places where traffickers are thought to exist, the thought of such teams operating on U.S. soil is in essence antithetical to the U.S. war machine. As scholars have noted "biopower and the sovereign right to kill are constitutive elements of modern state power … a state's monopoly on legitimate violence is essential to constructing the rationales of state security" (Rana 2011: 157).

Discursive slippages between the war on terror and the war on trafficking also persist in an effort to reify the two and build on both conversations to further "other" the figure of the Muslim. On September 4, 2011, popular CNN host Fareed Zakaria featured a roundtable to discuss the "troubling global status of women." Two of the three panelists were *New York Times* columnist Nicholas Kristof and his wife, Sheryl WuDunn, who together co-authored a book entitled *Half the Sky: Turning Oppression into Opportunity for Women.* Kristof, himself, is perhaps best known for his series of articles on sex trafficking in which he journeyed to Thailand to buy the freedom of a few young women in the sex industry. Scholars have written extensively on the problematic stance of Kristof (Bernstein 2007; Vance 2011; Peters 2010, personal communication) while follow-up articles have emphasized that some of these young women, whom Kristof refers to as "girls," have returned to the sex industry, not wanting to be freed or saved at all. Kristof has been joined on his crusade to save women around the world by his wife. Much of their work is about leveling criticism and accusation at Muslim majority countries, slipping between discourses about links between Islam and terror and Islam and trafficking. Their segment on Zakaria's show ended with an impassioned call to "bring the Muslim world out of the *dark ages*" (emphasis mine) as ostensibly, it is the Muslim world that presents women with their most pressing challenges. In the last few moments of the show, Kristof was unable to refrain from discussing trafficking, and he called up the "staggering scope of 'missing girls'" by referring to pictures of "missing girls on the back of milk cartons," reminding the world that now these girls are in faraway lands and need our help. Indeed, the saving trope is difficult to resist, however, the policies and efforts that have resulted from this sentiment have largely had negative consequences, not to mention the heavy impact of discourses such as those about the Muslim world being in the dark ages.

## Trafficking and Terror—The Securitization of Sexuality

As noted above, global trafficking rhetoric is inextricably tied to race—certain countries are castigated in the TIP report, and Muslim majority countries in particular are often painted as the source of the problem. Beyond the somewhat neocolonial intent manifest in the report lurks a moralized rhetoric about Muslim majority countries in particular that could be said to fuel a "clash of civilizations" (Huntington 1996). None of the "TIP heroes" of 2011 come from the Middle East or countries where Islam is the majority religion. Within Tier 3 rankings, the country narratives for Muslim majority countries such as Iran and Yemen stand in stark contrast to their fellow Tier 3 compatriots. For example, descriptions of sexual depravity (forced marriage of young girls, sexual exploitation of very young women, boys being sold into brothels, etc.) infuse the language explaining Iran's Tier 3 ranking, while the language about the Democratic Republic of Congo (also in Tier 3) focuses on labor abuses ("a significant number of miners—men and boys—are exploited in situations of debt bondage by businessmen"). Furthermore, the descriptions of the trafficking situation in places such as Iran are based on very little evidence. Buried in the third paragraph, the TIP authors admit that "lack of access to Iran by U.S. government officials impedes the collection of information on the country's human trafficking problem and the government's efforts to curb it," leaving us to question what the previous paragraphs—or even Tier 3 ranking—are based upon. Indeed, this brief sentence acknowledging a lack of information points to another major shortcoming of the report, namely the opaque nature of its compilation. The scope of the trafficking problems or governmental efforts to combat them is "not known" in several countries. In many of the country descriptions it is written that governments "seem" to be addressing the problem, while other countries "seem" not to be doing enough. What constitutes "enough," however, is not clear.

The gendering of the trafficking discourse focuses on women in the sex industry and is operationalized through a criminalization framework. This concentration on punishing the survivors rather than larger scope solutions is evident in the construction of policies such as the United Nations Palermo Protocol to Prevent, Suppress, and Punish Trafficking in Persons, *Especially Women and Children* (emphasis mine) which is housed in the United Nations Office on Drugs and Crime. Although the Palermo Protocol definition of trafficking is broad enough to encompass all instances of force, fraud, or coercion experienced by any person in any sector, the discursive focus is on women and children.[5] The U.S. Trafficking Victims Protection Act (TVPA n.d.), which forms the basis of the TIP, makes the connection more explicit by focusing on

---

5  Which enters the lexicon as womenandchildren, an infantilizing category. For more discussion of the women and children paradigm, see the work of Cynthia Enloe.

"women in the sex industry" as victims of *severe* trafficking (the only category demarcated as "deserving" protection in the form of a T-visa, a trafficking visa intended to assist and permit the survivor to remain in the United States). The approach taken to combat trafficking in these policies is threefold, as outlined by the TIP—prevention, protection, and prosecution—with an admitted focus on the latter category of prosecution.

The results of gender- and race-biased trafficking policies and discourse have been staggeringly negative, at least for places such as the United Arab Emirates. Women in the sex industry (regardless of whether they have experienced force, fraud, and coercion or not) are under hyperscrutiny and are subject to raids, arrests, and deportation—experiences that can feel more abusive than the ostensible force, fraud, or coercion they are thought to be experiencing. Women working in sex work (and even those thought to be working in the sex industry who may not be) are criminalized, as are those seeking to provide outreach to them within the prosecution paradigm. The experiences of men and women outside the sex industry who do experience abuse are eclipsed in this framing, perhaps most explicitly for men who are not at all imagined in the popular discourse as trafficked and thus unable to access any rights the framing might seek to offer. Recommendations to increase prosecutions and members of law enforcement (as was seen in Proposition 35) are problematic because of their potential to increase the amounts of abuse women experience. Many women I interviewed in Dubai, similar to what activists against Proposition 35 articulated, reported that it was the members of the imported law force[6] who were most often the source of abuse, while others described the experience of raids that followed the release of the TIP report each year as harrowing and abusive. The recommendation to tighten borders as well as ensuing policies in sending countries such as the Philippines (Philippines Household Reform Act of 2006) and Ethiopia also led to increasing problems for females who reported needing to migrate to make ends meet, but having to migrate through informal avenues which were often more abusive.

## Conclusion

In this era of globalization and postcolonial shifts, unfortunately, the larger public discourse and policy makers seem to be interested in over-simplified solutions to complex problems. In a recent conversation with a Washington, D.C.-based policy maker

---

6  In the UAE, because citizens make up such a small percentage of the population, the government must rely on imported migrants to meet the growing demands of law enforcement. Often these migrant law officers are not trained in working with survivors of trafficking and thus can be abusive. For more in-depth discussion of this see Mahdavi 2011.

working on human trafficking, I wondered aloud why the tropes cast by the U.S. wars on terror and trafficking were so powerful. "Because they are simple," was his response. "Because they show the public clearly who are the bad guys and who are the good guys, and they make our (U.S.) case for why we need to go after the bad guys really well," he added. But the problem is that these discourses are not aligned with reality and conspire to castigate a large segment of the world's population as either villains to be persecuted or victims to be saved; both constructed categories demand U.S. intervention.

Both the wars on terror and trafficking deploy macro level interventions (invading a country, and creating a report whereby *countries* are responsible for combatting trafficking) to address what are portrayed as individual (or micro) failings, shortcomings, and challenges. Rings of organized crime are narrated as the source of both terrorism and trafficking. This portraiture is problematic in that states are blamed for (what are seen as) individual failings within their borders. Simultaneously, the role of states in structuring policies and developing postcolonial political economic systems that exacerbate inequalities and result in migrants needing to cross borders to make ends meet is eclipsed.

The paradigm of human trafficking, which remains part of a larger conversation seeking to account for and respond to particular aspects of human mobility at the beginning of the 21st century, must remain dynamic and flexible if it is to prove relevant to policy makers, advocates, and citizens of the world. If the concept remains myopically centered around unrealistic, over-individualistic ideas of migration rooted in a force/choice dichotomy, it will prove increasingly irrelevant to lived experiences of migrants. Individual agency and personal decision-making must be accounted for and contextualized within comprehensive analyses of the macro, structural elements shaping migration, citizenship, and statehood at the global, regional, and state levels. It is the stories of migrants, contrasted with the way in which the public narrates their experiences, that will enable us to have a more robust conversation about the realities of the challenges facing migrants. Understanding the construction of discourse and the perpetuation of moral crusades is the first step in considering the environment structuring the lived realities of migrants and Muslims today.

## DISCUSSION QUESTIONS

1. How are the wars on terror and trafficking examples of moral crusades?
2. What are some of the negative results of the moral panic around trafficking? Around terrorism?
3. How do we see a disconnect between policy and lived experience manifested in the war on terror and the war on trafficking?

# II: Colliding Wars

On April 27, 2012, Google Ideas, the "think/do tank" of Google Inc., hosted a roundtable in conjunction with the Council on Foreign Relations (CFR) wherein policy experts and think tankers from Washington, D.C., New York, and across the globe were convened. The theme of the roundtable was "Illicit Networks: Mafia States and Nonstate Actors" and was part of a larger initiative investigating the role technology plays in fueling or fighting four areas of illicit networks that Google chose to focus on: human trafficking, arms smuggling, drug trafficking, and organ trafficking. The initiative focusing on illicit networks culminated in a summit held in July of the same year.

The roundtable focused on the role of ambiguously categorized weak states in fueling trafficking. Not only were the contours of what makes a weak state not defined, but many of the participants were counterterrorism experts who drew on terrorism rhetoric to bolster their arguments about certain states exacerbating the problem of trafficking. What was most starkly manifest in this panel was the dearth of expertise on the intersection of technology and trafficking acknowledged by many of the participants themselves. Weak or failing states such as Afghanistan, Burma, North Korea, Iran, Syria, and Tunisia were all named as areas of insecurity for the speakers who pointed to these states as sources of the problem of illicit networks. Some analysts pointed to the possibility of organized crime syndicates taking over entire states and encouraging illicit activities such as human, arms, and drug trafficking. Others spoke of the corruptibility of the governments of these weak states, thus resulting in a need to monitor these governments closely. Two participants specifically contended that the governments of weak states were members of organized crime and illicit networks. Three other participants could not resist linking trafficking and terror, arguing that mafia states are breeding grounds of both terrorism and trafficking, and that the same networks that fund one often fund the other.

Two days earlier, Google Ideas hosted a different panel with the New York-based Tribeca Film Festival, its other partner on the project. The purpose of the Google/ Tribeca panel was to investigate the role of film and documentaries in framing the issues bound up in illicit networks. The panel was comprised of survivors of different types of illicit networks, including a survivor of forced labor, a former arms smuggler, a former child soldier, and a survivor of sex trafficking. The survivors spoke to the disconnect between film portrayals of their lives and the realities of living inside these networks. It was a powerful moment for members of the audience who were organizers of the Tribeca Film Festival, actors, directors, producers, and other members of the film industry, who began to think differently about their overly simplistic conceptions of human trafficking and arms smuggling.

Several things bear mentioning about these two events, and the timing, location, and composition of the panels exemplifies the pervasiveness of a paradigm. To begin, the organization and convening of the panels shows the involvement of several discourse leaders (which I will refer to as sectors) in the issues surrounding trafficking, namely: Washington (the CFR and many participants on the mafia states roundtable), Wall Street (the investors and capital behind the events), Hollywood (Tribeca and other members of the film industry), and most recently Silicon Valley (Google). That these different sectors have all sought involvement in the issues has been cause for alarm for some and celebration for others. And, in fact, it is possible that this involvement is a cause for both. What is important to recognize, however, is the reality, which is that they have all decided to engage with the topic—making them now stakeholders—and they are each discourse makers in their various ways. We need to understand the power of each sector, and the ways in which these discourse leaders have structured a paradigm in order to deconstruct the easy slippage of trafficking and terror, and victims and villains, while examining the construction of the phrase "illicit networks."

Recognizing that these four sectors (Washington, Wall Street, Hollywood, and Silicon Valley) have significant overlap and often shared ventures and understanding that each sector is by no means monolithic, I would like to examine each group separately in order to demonstrate ways each has contributed to the construction of the paradigms that have sutured or fused together trafficking and terror. While these are not the only nor primary stakeholders in structuring the discourses around trafficking and/or terror, I feel that the nexus of these sectors, and the way in which each contributes to the moral crusade merits close examination.[1] I will look at the stakeholders in each group, and explore how rhetoric about race, class, and sexuality feeds into the construction of the paradigm. Similar to ways in which the trafficking discourse has wedded women and children to the point where the turn of phrase has entered the lexicon as "womenandchildren," we see a similar suturing of trafficking and terror to the extent where the two are viewed as one. Following on feminist scholar and activist Cynthia Enloe's construction of womenandchildren, therefore, I have fused traffickingandterror to indicate the discursive turn of the phrase that has led to both paradigms and policies that often erroneously link terrorists and traffickers.

Collapsing the wars on terror and trafficking into a traffickingandterror paradigm conflates the bad guys of terrorism with the bad guys of trafficking and creates a racialized and sexualized stereotype. Notably, it further reifies the "othering" process,

---

1. Elizabeth Bernstein and others have written extensively about the role of right-wing and Christian Evangelical organizations in attempting to frame both the trafficking debate and outcomes.

or the construction of a different, and possibly dangerous "other," which legitimates intervention. If an "other" can be constructed and fetishized, as Edward Said argues in his groundbreaking book *Orientalism* (1978)[2] then violence against an "other," constructed as a bad guy, seems less obtrusive. Collapsing terror and trafficking constructs the image of a bad guy in need of monitoring and surveillance (though what form this surveillance takes is deliberately left opaque). When the discourse presumes that a person involved in terror could and would be involved in trafficking (without any interrogation of whether this is in fact true), a particular bad guy is constructed who appears capable of all nefarious activities ranging from terror to kidnapping and trafficking persons globally—thus the creation of a moral crusade to save the world from the bad guys.

The second function of the traffickingandterror paradigm is the portraiture of the "other" as hypersexualized and deviant. In their brilliant piece, *Monster, Terrorist, Fag*, Jasbir Puar and Amit Rai (2002) argue that one form of framing certain Muslims as terrorists or possible terrorists is the construction of their sexualities as deviant and in need of control or monitoring. Puar (2007) points to the Abu Ghraib incident, where U.S. military personnel attempted to sexually shame Arab prisoners publicly, as an example of a hypersexualization of the "other." Furthermore, Joseph Massad and others have shown that the discourse about homosexuality in the Middle East feeds into this same rhetoric of wanting to "otherize": or prove Middle Eastern sexualities as deviant, fetishized, lacking, and possibly dangerous.[3] The portraitures of Middle Eastern sexualities can be curiously in contradiction with one another; their deviance (read: dangerous tendencies in need of Western control) is characterized as either submissive/homosexual, or as lecherous/hypersexualized. Both depictions are "other"ing and both depictions are linked with a justification and a moral obligation for the West to interfere in Middle Eastern political as well as *personal* life. At Abu Ghraib, Iraqi prisoners were forced and humiliated by U.S. troops to portray submissive and homosexual acts, which reinforced the trope of Middle Eastern deviance and the depiction of terrorists as homosexuals (in contrast to the masculine U.S. troops); it also resulted in a reactionary discourse by journalists and others that pointed to the torture as exceptionally humiliating for Middle Eastern men because the Middle East was host to a repressed society with "perversity bubbling just beneath the surface" (Puar 2007: 525). Thus this discourse surrounding the scandal reinforces the trope of hypersexualized Middle Eastern men in need of control. As Puar writes, "at the heart of Orientalist notions of sexuality is the paradoxical view that the Orient is both the space of 'illicit and dangerous sex' and the site of carefully suppressed animalistic instincts" (Puar 2007: 526).

---

2. For further reading on the concept of "Orientalism," see the work of Joseph Massad.

3. For further information, see the work of Jasbir Puar, Joseph Massad, or Ghassan Makarem.

The Middle Eastern terrorist, also conflated with the "brown" trafficker, is constructed as dangerous through these depictions of sexual perversity, which include "failed heterosexuality, Western notions of the psyche, and a certain queer monstrosity" (Puar and Rai 2002: 117). The Western discourses about homosexuality in the Middle East are just as conflicted as the discourses surrounding the hypersexualized and lecherous side of the construct. On the one hand, the Middle East is cast as deviant for its lack of tolerance towards homosexuality (pitting the backward Middle East against the progressive and tolerant West), but on the other hand, men's gender performativity, if slightly outside the paradigm of male gender performativity in the West, becomes pointed to as homosexuality, in a homophobic way. As Massad (2007) points out, the main flaws with Western conceptualizations of Middle Eastern sexuality are that they are (1) ahistorical, (2) painted as monolithic across the region, and (3) presuppose a Western binary of gay/straight when this binary does not necessarily translate.

The tropes, or metaphors and stereotypes, about human trafficking have focused on the sex industry as discussed in the previous chapter. Therefore, collapsing terror and trafficking further castigates the sexualities of terrorists or possible terrorists as deviant. Assuming that trafficking is a problem particularly linked to networks of organized crime involved in terrorism racializes the issue, and sexualizes those presumed to be terrorists. This sexual "othering" further fuels Islamophobia and bolsters the moral crusade against Muslims.

This chapter examines ways in which discourses and paradigms about traffickingandterror have been produced, taken root, and gained power, especially in a post-9/11, post-TVPA moment in the United States. I describe how various discourse makers have promulgated the moral panic surrounding weak states and their culpability in promoting traffickingandterror. The impact of the various sectors will be assessed as well as the larger impact on particular populations who have already been made vulnerable by both the wars on terror and trafficking including migrants, Muslims, and sex workers.

## Washington—Misconnections and Misportrayals

I will now return to an analysis of the "Illicit Networks: Mafia States and Nonstate Actors" roundtable because several dimensions of the focus on the constructed categories of weak or mafia states require further scrutiny. First, the conversation focused largely on the role of weak states in fueling illicit networks. The definition of a weak state was left unclear, and as the discussion ensued, weak states seemed to refer to states that were not reliable allies with the United States such as Iran, North Korea, Afghanistan, and Burma (rather than simply less developed states). Other weak states included Tunisia and many parts of the Middle East post-Arab Spring of 2010. Several speakers referred to the Arab Spring on more than one occasion because these particular weak states were perceived as breeding grounds of terrorism.

The focus of the roundtable was supposed to be on "illicit networks" (although this term was also deliberately left vague), primarily human and organ trafficking. As previously stated, the speakers, however (ironically), were not trafficking experts, but rather counterterrorism gurus. One participant who reflected on the panel some weeks later noted, "When the first speaker said 'human trafficking is a big problem in Burma,' I was shocked, because I thought, wow, that is the first time the words human trafficking have come out of that guy's mouth." Another panel participant reflected, "It was almost as if they just took out the word 'terrorism' from all their speeches and papers and just inserted the word 'trafficking' without really thinking about it. It's the panic *du jour*." Noted counterterrorism experts filled the room, but the focus of the conversation was on trafficking as opposed to terrorism.

While human trafficking was discussed extensively, many of the panelists had not done actual research on trafficking, and the inadvertent slip to terrorism proved too tempting for the panelists. The two terms were conflated, and "weak" or "mafia" states were blamed. No one brought up an interrogation of the terms "weak" or "mafia" state. And no one acknowledged that trafficking and in fact illicit networks writ large (1) take place around the world regardless of the type of state and (2) that the category "illicit" presupposes a bifurcation of licit and illicit and ignores the fact that the two are closely intertwined and often dependent on one another. Furthermore, the conversation focused on illicit networks as an inherently modern day problem intensifying each day, largely due to the presence of terrorism.

This focus on the new and threatening phenomenon of illicit networks obscures, the fact that informal economies and illicit trade has occurred across the globe throughout history. As noted scholar Peter Andreas (2011) has extensively documented, all forms of illicit exchange from humans to drugs have transpired since at least the 1400s if not further back in history. As Andreas observes, Charles Dickens complained for many years that publishers in the United States were illegally selling his books without his permission because the copyright laws in the United Kingdom did not extend outside national borders. To further the point, Andreas points to the British East India Company as a type of transnational organized crime conglomerate who monopolized the production and trade of opium throughout the 18th century. When counterterrorism experts in Washington claim, in an ahistorical fashion, that trafficking is a problem today because of terrorism, they neglect the important fact that trafficking has a long history of moral panic, dating back to the white slave trade, and therefore cannot be the fault simply of particular weak or failing states.

What makes a country a weak or mafia state is unclear, especially given that criminal networks pervade all types of countries regardless of their development status. In my analysis of the conversation above and in the clamoring calls from Washington, it seems as though so-called mafia states are often Muslim countries. As one Washington official told me, places such as Iran or Syria are seen as vulnerable to organized crime of a "different and dangerous level." When a participant at the roundtable brought up

Italy as the first place he thought of when hearing the phrase "mafia state," his remark was scoffed at and dismissed.

Furthermore, the ostensible focus on the undefined category of weak states presupposes a hierarchy wherein some states are strong, presumably the more developed states. What is missing from this analysis, however, is the role of developed states and transnational organizations, such as the International Monetary Fund or World Bank. These institutions (or organizations) are heavily influenced by certain strong states in furthering a geopolitical economy that continues to favor some markets and some states over others. The presumed threat of weak states obscures the role of strong states and neocolonialism in producing a political economy that leaves some countries less developed than others. When the impact of Structural Adjustment Programs of lending and debt structured by the IMF and World Bank are considered, the impact of strong states on weak nations becomes clearer (Mahdavi 2011).

Beyond the isolated incident of the roundtable described above, Washington's message about Muslim countries perceived to be weak or mafia states is reflected in global reports such as the Trafficking in Persons report (TIP). In a perpetual cycle, discourse is both active in influencing policy makers and reactive to policies already created, thus manifesting the fact that discourse shapes and is shaped by policy. That a Muslim country might be a best practice model within the TIP seems to be out of the range of possibilities as TIP heroes almost never come from the Muslim world. The one time that a TIP hero did come from the United Arab Emirates, it was an American woman named Sharla Musabih, who had married an Emirati, set up a shelter, but was later convicted of trafficking the women she claimed to protect.[4] In conversations with various TIP officers, the one theme that emerges repeatedly is the need to rescue and save women in the Middle East who are particularly vulnerable. The possibility that Muslim women or men in a particular country might be working on empowerment programs is not considered by those officials who have not recognized the local grassroots activism currently taking place to empower women, migrants, and other vulnerable populations in the Middle East.[5]

Discourse and policy are intricately interconnected as discourse and paradigms which can take the form of moral crusades can affect how policies are operationalized. The examples above of the TIP, the TVPA, and even the Palermo Protocol illustrate this in great detail. Palermo operates out of a criminalization framework manifest in its location in the United Nations Office on Drugs and Crime, and the focus of both the TVPA and TIP[6] is on prosecution rather than protection or prevention. Recall that prosecution is a large part of the justification for assigning a particular ranking. This

---

4  For further information see Mahdavi 2011.

5  For more discussion of this important area of inquiry, see Sajoo 2004.

6  Not unlike that of Proposition 35 in California and even the white slave trade of the 19th century.

hyperfocus on crime and criminalization synchronizes easily with language about the mafia and organized crime or mafia states. This focus on the larger state and crime units, of course, obscures the fact that in reality much of trafficking involves family members, or persons known to the migrants.

The language and policies employed to fuel a morally infused framework depicts a series of bad guys whose power needs to be controlled. How they are to be controlled is deliberately left ambiguous. When Washington-based think tank strategists and journalists such as Moisés Naím (whose *Foreign Affairs* article "The Rise of the Mafia State" generated much conversation and was touted as a major prediction about the future of foreign policy) write about their worry that law enforcement cannot keep up with organized crime, the implied message is that law enforcement needs to be given more power, and perhaps we need to have more military spending, rather than assessing the social and economic factors that lead to decisions that can make persons or states vulnerable.

Perhaps the most confusing fact about both the roundtable and articles such as the Moisés Naím piece is that, after making a series of statements fueling moral panic about the terrorandtrafficking threat, the resounding conclusion asserted by the participants and the Naím piece was simply that data were needed. Buried in the analysis of experts who make conjectures about the fate of countries based on assumptions is the fact that data to support the claims are hard to collect. This begs the question: upon what data is the analysis just presented based? Indeed, the Routes Project (Howard and Traughber 2007), one of the few endeavors to collect data on the nexus of trafficking and terror, concluded that there are no data to show this connection in at least four regions that were surveyed—the Caucasus, Georgia, Central Asia, and South Eastern Europe. Most authors on the Routes Project determined that there was a lack of sufficient connections between terrorism and human trafficking other than correlational data which claimed that terrorists and traffickers use the same routes to engage in their illicit activities. While there was determined to be somewhat of a link between arms and drug trafficking and terrorism, all data was similarly based on correlational conjectures rather than a concrete analysis taking both terrorism and trafficking into account.

The problem with the rhetoric bolstering the moral crusade against terrorandtrafficking is that assumptions and conjectures are made about what needs to be done to combat these weak states, rather than suggesting ways to generate and find the data that would support these claims. Missteps of policies that are disconnected from lived reality can often prove tragic. In order to bring policy in line with lived reality, data drawn from lived realities of those most affected by illicit networks and the ensuing policies, need to be brought to the table in Washington and the other sectors. Both qualitative and quantitative data amassed from interviews and surveys with persons living inside and affected by policies on illicit networks can help illuminate the contours of challenges faced by those in need. Currently, scholars are working within various sectors of labor migration (Parrenas, Constable, Friedman, Yeoh, Gupta), human trafficking (Brennan, Cheng, Bernstein, Vance, Saunders, Haynes, Burke, Jordan), labor exploitation (Skinner, Gardner, Nguyen, Ong), and other types of networks to bring lived experience to light. The work of these scholars can be helpful in igniting more robust conversations that are based on data as opposed to conjecture.

## Wall Street—Financing Fear

Wall Street, an alias for large corporate investment and involvement, has recently had an interest in funding and promulgating both the discourse on trafficking that focuses on sex trafficking, as well as the moral panic from Washington and Hollywood that links trafficking and terror. Through funding initiatives such as Siddharth Kara's research on trafficking in brothels, the International Justice Mission, or the Not For Sale Campaign, many big banks and corporations have tried to demonstrate their commitment to fighting trafficking by focusing on the sex industry. For example, major corporations such as Google have donated hundreds of thousands of dollars towards organizations like the International Justice Mission in an effort to curb trafficking and slavery in foreign nations. When Wall Street tycoon Swanee Hunt began pushing her end demand strategy of ending trafficking through ending demand for sex work (or prostitution, as she characterizes it), the response of Wall Street was almost audible. Several groups rushed to fund her initiative, not recognizing the inherent downfalls of the end demand strategy, nor the problematic nature of framing trafficking as an issue rooted in the sex industry.

Elizabeth Bernstein and others have carefully documented the pitfalls inherent to the end demand model. Beyond the' framing of trafficking as an issue only in the sex industry (Hunt and her friends are not proposing we end demand for sweaters or rugs made by forced labor, fish caught by men in bondage on fishing boats, or that we end demand for domestic work), the presupposition that ending demand for sex is possible or will diminish trafficking is demonstrably false. The main source of data to support this approach has been what proponents refer to as "the Swedish Model." Bernstein, in a multi-site study of Sweden, San Francisco, and Amsterdam, has shown ways in which the Swedish model actually made women in the sex industry *more* vulnerable, all the while failing to address or decrease trafficking. Bernstein notes that when end demand was operationalized in Sweden, clients and sex workers were driven further underground, and sex workers reported that the new policies made it more difficult to screen their clients to keep themselves safe. More of the transactions were taking place underground, and some women with limited options chose to migrate to other countries to engage in sex work, rendering them more vulnerable (Bernstein 2007).

Part of the end demand strategy encapsulates harsh punishment of "johns" or clients. In San Francisco, they are sent to "john schools" where they are told about the harmful effects of their activities. Beyond funding end demand efforts, other members of Wall Street have become actively involved in these efforts through new program initiatives. One example is the work of major Wall Street player, a large transnational bank, who has launched a program to track credit card purchases of its clients in order to assist in finding and prosecuting persons thought to be spending money in unethical ways. When asked to elaborate on these unethical ways, one person involved in the campaign said that this terminology was in reference to "nefarious activity such as human trafficking or terrorism. We are trying to figure out how terrorists and traffickers use and move money. Since we can track their credit cards, we can follow the money and follow their movement."

Similar to the paradigm of traffickingandterror that is espoused by Washington, Wall Street has capitalized on the same paradigms of villain and victim, to justify its involvement in programs such as the one outlined above, as well as its support of end demand. Furthermore, when end demand is the focus, and the spotlight shines on sex trafficking, instances of abuse outside the sex industry are eclipsed. Wall Street has a vested interest in rehearsing paradigms shaped by both Washington and Hollywood that focus on particular bad guys, terrorists, weak states, or nefarious "johns." This focus on weak states or terrorists as the source of the problem, like the focus on sex work, obscures the role of corporations, capitalist structures, and the political economy in fueling inequality, forced labor, and **structural violence**. Elsewhere I have elaborated on the role of corporations in promoting structural violence (Mahdavi 2011), therefore here, I would like to point to a more specific example of the role of Wall Street and corporations in fostering an environment where persons are vulnerable to trafficking.

It is no secret that globalization and political economic structures that promote capitalism depend on a flexible oversupply of labor and a race to the bottom in terms of prices for goods, services, and most recently labor (Marx and Engels 1848/1969; Mitchell 2011). The demand for cheap goods and products has led many corporations to become reliant upon offshore labor activities that lend themselves to the force, fraud, or coercion that undergirds human trafficking. In a news story published in *Bloomberg BusinessWeek* on February 23, 2012 by author and investigative journalist Ben Skinner, he revealed that several major U.S. conglomerates and corporations including P.F. Chang's, Walmart, and Costco were buying and serving seafood caught on a particular fishing boat off the coast of New Zealand. Fishermen on this boat were mostly from Indonesia or South Korea, and were forced to work 30–35 hour shifts, in unsafe and substandard work conditions.

Skinner put me in contact with three of the fishermen who had left the boat and returned to their homes in West Java. When I asked them about their experiences, they were very forthcoming: "We were treated like animals, like dogs. They kicked us. We worked more than 24 hours. We couldn't see. And after many months, we did not get our money" (interview, May 15, 2012). When Skinner exposed the role of U.S.

corporations in buying seafood from this particular Korean-run ship, little changed in the United States. However, the fishermen who had come forward were sent home without their wages, and they are currently working odd jobs on local boats in West Java, just trying to catch enough fish to feed their families.

This case demonstrates the central role of corporations in human trafficking—a part of the story that is very rarely told. That corporations and capitalist forces rely on a flexible oversupply of cheap labor to remain competitive in the market place is accepted without much questioning of the type of force, fraud, or coercion these unethical labor practices can produce. While Skinner exposed this one link in the supply chain of major corporations, there are many more that remain undocumented and unnoticed. Furthermore, these instances are rarely thought of as trafficking, given the gendered nature of the trafficking paradigm that typically focuses exclusively on women in the sex industry. Elsewhere (Mahdavi 2011) I have detailed the responses of audiences, policy makers, and NGO personnel when I mention trafficked men or forced labor. Respondents are often incredulous, and responses include, "men aren't trafficked," or "they are better off in these situations so it's ok," or "they wanted to get work and so it's not trafficking." Forced labor, regardless of gender, race, or industry, is absolutely a case of human trafficking. It is in the interest of major corporations, however, to keep the focus of human trafficking on the sex industry so that they can continue these damaging labor practices with less scrutiny.

For this reason, Wall Street, along with Washington and Hollywood, has continued to produce and support projects and paradigms that focus either on the sex industry, or on particular bad guys or weak states. The traffickingandterror framework, therefore, works in their favor, as they are able to evade focus on their own murky activities in order to remain competitive, keep product prices down, and continue the global race to the bottom not only for goods, but also for labor.

## Hollywood—Producing Panics

The film industry's continual production and promotion of paradigms that link trafficking and terror takes many forms. The most obvious role of this particular sector is the production of films and television shows that play into and help reinforce particular tropes. From the films *Taken* to *Call and Response* to *Human Trafficking* to the TV series *Missing*, human trafficking is typically portrayed by Hollywood's biggest blockbusters with a recurring script: a young white girl is taken or kidnapped, forced into sex slavery, often by dark skinned men with Middle Eastern accents, for the benefit of nefarious men who speak other languages, are accepted to be patriarchal, or are members of organized crime rings and networks. The messages implied by Hollywood are in line with Washington and Wall Street human trafficking: (1) is always about forcing young girls into the sex industry, (2) is usually masterminded by people other than Americans (typically Muslim looking/sounding or other types of terrorists), and (3) is a problem of organized crime.

Few films present a storyline or message that is more complex or nuanced. Hollywood films bear little resemblance to the lived experience of many migrants other than sex workers. Rarely do you see a film depicting a young man who was encouraged by his family, and made a difficult decision to leave home to support his loved ones but was abused when arriving in the new work place. The films that supposedly shed light on the underground lives of traffickers and trafficking have all done exceedingly well, both on the big screen and on television. Not only have they generated large profits and viewership, but these films are often pointed to by policy makers and other discourse leaders as proof of the contours of the trafficking framework.

*Mammoth,* a small budget film by Lukas Moodysson, is one of the rare exceptions to the films mentioned above. This film depicts the global interconnections of labor, sexuality, race, class, and gender, and is not thought to be a film about trafficking, as the term is not explicitly mentioned in the title or script. Instead, the film features three different families in three different countries who have become connected through the flow of migrant labor. The main family lives in New York City and is comprised of Ellen, an emergency room doctor (played by Michelle Williams), Leo, a video game engineer (played by Gael Garcia Bernal), and their eight-year-old daughter. Also living in their house is Gloria, their nanny, who has left her two sons in the care of her own mother back in the Philippines so that she can migrate to the United States to care for Ellen and Leo's daughter while they work long hours.

In this film, Leo travels to Thailand to broker a deal for his video game company. Bored by the minutia of business deals, he decides to travel to a small island in search of adventure. When he arrives, he meets Cookie, a Thai woman working in the sex industry who expresses interest in Leo. We see the complex interconnections of the characters' lives. Ellen feels frustrated by her lack of parenting skills with her daughter and takes her anger out on Gloria, who already is working long days with very few breaks (when the little girl is at school, Gloria is shown scrubbing toilets and cooking and cleaning). Simultaneously, Gloria's family back in the Philippines suffers from her absence as her eight-year-old son attempts to make money to bring her back home but is raped and abused by an Australian sex tourist in the process. Meanwhile, Leo becomes romantically involved with Cookie, who is hoping he gives her enough money to send home to her mother who is caring for her one-year-old baby. As the film ends, Gloria quits her job in New York to go back to her family when she learns her son has been hospitalized. Ellen is forced to stay home and bond with her daughter, while Leo leaves Cookie in the middle of the night with a parting gift of a mammoth bone pen, which is worth thousands of dollars in the United States but for which Cookie can only get $15 to send home to her daughter. Cookie had thought that Leo agreed to help support her, but instead, she was left with a pen.

The characters in this film are not explicitly forced, frauded, or coerced. But many of them have been forced to choose (Doezema 2005) from a series of difficult options. Gloria, for example, must leave her children behind in the Philippines to work long hours caring for other people's children across the globe. Ellen and Cookie also find themselves forced to choose between families and work in very different circumstances. What the film portrays with careful precision is the complex decision-making processes that many people face in order to support their families or careers.

It also demonstrates that people can get into difficult situations without the involvement of particular bad guys or terrorists. Political economy and structural violence in the form of failing economies, or employment opportunities that favor certain genders, classes, or races can often be the bad guys that force people to choose from a limited series of options. While this film is richly detailed and brings to light the complexities inherent in leading to trafficking-like situations, it was neither wildly successful at the box office, nor is it identified by policy makers as a film that examines different issues of force, fraud, or coercion that can take place within labor and migration.

In general, the issue of forced labor, and the kinds of labor that can fall into the continuum and spectrum of forced, is very rarely addressed by Hollywood. This omission was made further evident by the Google/Tribeca panel described at the opening of this chapter. The goal of the panel was to reveal the disconnect between film portrayals of illicit networks such as human, drug, and arms trafficking, and the lived experiences within these spheres. During the panel, the moderator would show a clip from a film and then ask the survivor to explain whether the film got it right. For example, the film *Blood Diamond* was shown, and then Okello Sam, a former child soldier, was asked to comment on its accuracy. The films *Trade* and *Hustle and Flow* were shown and "T," a survivor of sex trafficking, was asked to comment on both. Tellingly, one of the survivors, "G" did not have any film to which to respond. He is a survivor of labor trafficking who had worked in the agrcultural industry in the U.S. and been repeatedly abused by his employer.

It is telling that Google and Tribeca together had not been able to find a single film that showed any type of force, fraud, or coercion outside the sex industry. Furthermore, "G's" stories of his compatriots for whose rights he now fights, did not speak to the far-reaching arms of organized crime or terrorists who might have funded the illicit networks in which he was involved. Rather, he explained that most people entered the agriculture industry through family contacts and were abused by a series of employers. In a subsequent interview after the panel, "G" expressed frustration at the composition of the event; he felt that he was not able to articulate the context and complexity of the problem. "G's" experiences are outside the paradigms of good guys and bad guys and traffickingandterror produced by Hollywood, and thus he felt that his narrative was difficult to convey to the gathered audience. The panel was an important and powerful turning point for many of the discourse makers in the room because it challenged them to ask themselves why this dimension of the human trafficking was missing from their frame of analysis.

In addition to the role of films in producing paradigms, is the role of Hollywood stars and starlets in leading particular campaigns to fight trafficking. Among those who have been particularly vocal on the topic of human trafficking are Mira Sorvino, Ashton Kutcher, Demi Moore, Julia Ormond, and Ashely Judd. With the exception of Julia Ormond, who only recently has started speaking out about forced labor, all of these Hollywood stars focus on the topic of sex trafficking, and recycle the script presented in many of the blockbusters described above. Ashton Kutcher and Demi Moore started the DNA Foundation to promote the end demand strategy as described earlier in the chapter. To promote the foundation's work Kutcher's "Real Men Don't Buy Girls" campaign, premised on his message that trafficking could come to an end if men didn't buy girls, came to a tragic end when Kutcher was found to (1) be cheating on his wife with many girls, and (2) came out in support of Joe Paterno, the Pennsylvania State University football coach who was fired for not taking stronger action in the case of Jerry Sandusky, an assistant coach found guilty of engaging in sexual harassment of young males. This also followed the Bill Hillar scandal detailed in the first chapter, while coming on the heels of Kutcher and Moore's very public divorce.

Mira Sorvino (who starred in *Human Trafficking*) and Ashely Judd (who was featured in *Missing*) both continue to make public statements in the same vein as the storylines in their respective films. In interviews (such as with CNN's Jim Clancey, Oct. 5, 2012), Sorvino speaks only about young girls who were kidnapped or tricked and sold into sex slavery. In her narrative, the demarcations between bad guys and good guys are quite clear, and there is very little room for nuance. Her insistence on only using the word "victim" also feeds into a victimological approach, wherein the women are portrayed as one-dimensional and further stripped of their agency. Furthermore, she narrates a desire to save the girls she meets in shelters in many parts of the developing world, which feeds raced rhetoric about white women needing to save brown women from brown men (Abu-Lughod 2002; Spivak 2006). Similarly, Ashley Judd writes in her bio that she has always had "an intense sense of righteous indignation and urge to speak for the voiceless and oppressed" (700 Club n.d.). That the described "voiceless and oppressed" need her to save them is also problematic, as is her description about an incident that piqued her interest in human trafficking. When she visited Thailand in 2004, she "listened to the stories of six prostitutes living there—and became desperate to help them escape" (700 Club n.d.). Whether or not these women wanted to leave the sex industry is unclear, and whether or not they were trafficked is not known, but rather assumed by Judd. She expresses a passion to save them from themselves without learning the complexities of their lived experiences.

While it is admirable that Hollywood stars have an interest in these issues and wish to dedicate their time to traveling the world and speaking out about the perils of human trafficking, it is important that they recognize the power of their actions and speech. The way they discuss and frame an issue becomes accepted as discourse while bolstering a larger moral crusade. Furthermore, their focus on sex trafficking obscures other types of trafficking as well as the systemic causes that render persons vulnerable. Thus, they can inadvertently reinforce policies and campaigns that harm rather than help those most affected by the challenges inherent in forced labor and migration.

Finally, by dividing the world into distinct categories of good guys and bad guys, they participate in the creation and perpetuation of discourse about certain populations (usually raced and gendered) as a threat and requiring monitoring or surveillance. These good versus bad categories, which also imply the need for moral interference in addition to state control, further bolster the traffickingandterror frame.

## Silicon Valley; Reprogramming Paradigms

Silicon Valley (a blanket term applying to some of the world's largest technology companies such as Microsoft, Facebook, Twitter, Google, and others) seems to be the newest player to the table in producing or interrogating paradigms about the wars on trafficking, terror, and the trope of traffickingandterror. Although late in joining the debate, the companies served as arbiters and conveners in bringing together the different sectors. This has been the cause of both worry and hope for members in other sectors as well as academics, practitioners, and survivors who are currently assessing this newcomer to see whether technology will ultimately be used in positive or negative ways. Perhaps the most positive aspect of the involvement of Silicon Valley is that the companies haven't followed the lead of the previous sectors, and have not been as quick to cast the players involved in trafficking as good and bad guys. Instead, they want to investigate and focus just on trafficking (though many of them continue to view trafficking through a criminalization frame, and some remain focused on sex trafficking), while being careful not to conflate trafficking and terrorism.

Because nearly everyone relies on technology, and because of the image projected by many tech companies as being cutting edge and committed to many different issues (see Google, Facebook, Microsoft), they have the power to bring many players to the table. Through organizing events, summits, and conferences (like the two described at the beginning of the chapter), launching initiatives (such as Microsoft's request for proposals investigating the Role of Technology in Human Trafficking), and funding campaigns (such as Facebook, Microsoft, and Twitter's support of the group Stop Child Sex Trafficking Now), technology groups have demonstrated that they can operate unilaterally and multilaterally to fund conversations, projects, and research on this issue. Though some of the involvement has been through philanthropic arms of the tech groups (like Google.org funding the International Justice Mission or Polaris

Project in setting up a national human trafficking hotline), this sector has increasingly wanted to get involved in more far-reaching ways by looking at the role of technology in fueling and fighting human trafficking.

Some of the initiatives launched by various tech companies have the power to address the challenges inherent to forced labor and migration in far reaching ways. Furthermore, tech companies are emerging as major discourse makers, and therefore the messages that they send can be a powerful force for social change. Currently, the projects that are being launched could be read as tools of empowerment, or optics of surveillance. Some examples of these projects include (1) Microsoft's initiative to understand the Role of Technology in Human Trafficking, (2) Google Ideas' most recent project looking at the role of technology in promoting or fighting illicit networks, and (3) Lexis-Nexis using its search capabilities and extensive database to document and search the presence of trafficking online. How they will further be operationalized remains to be seen. While the crowdsourcing mechanisms proposed or inferred from some of these programs might be a violation of privacy, these companies are also exploring how technology can be used as a platform for migrants to communicate, transmit information, and empower one another to leave situations that violate their rights. Grassroots groups have been in conversation with tech companies to talk about the creation of free and supported "bad date lists" which transmit information about clients, services and outreach to sex workers in local, national, and transnational contexts. Other activists have proposed solutions such as recycling cell phones that would allow migrants in developing countries to receive information via text messaging. Overall, the fact that those with the lived experience are coming to the table and talking with members of Silicon Valley is a positive sign. It is also of note that the tech companies have worked diligently not to reproduce the traffickingandterror paradigm, even if they slip into the rhetoric at occasional events. The initiatives put forward have been about addressing problems of trafficking *or* terrorism, which is further cause for hope.

## Interconnections, Incomplete Conclusions

Because the way in which we conceptualize murky concepts such as trafficking, terrorism, or weak states forms the basis not only for how policies are written, but also how they are operationalized, it is important to have a strong understanding of these paradigms. Examining various stakeholders gives us a better sense of what the paradigms are, how they are constructed and produced, how pervasive they are, and their impact on lived experience. Most notably, the perpetuation of a linked and reified traffickingandterror discourse has resulted in further acceptance of Islamophobia and a fueling of clash of civilizations (Huntington 1996) type rhetoric. If it is accepted that the main challenges facing our world today come from particular weak states that are breeding grounds for traffickingandterror, then the deployment of any means necessary to contain these states becomes legitimated. Furthermore, the role of strong states in either trafficking or terror is eclipsed, as is the role of corporations and other key players and events structuring our current geopolitical moment. The focus on organized crime or particular nefarious networks that trade in both terror and trafficking once again places the spotlight on the Muslim world, which is generally accepted (through mainstream Hollywood portrayals and Washington-based discourse) to be the heart of these crimes. This focus allows for any type of intervention in places seen as the heart of darkness and encourages human trafficking policies, which are supposed to protect the rights of vulnerable populations, to be used as anti-immigration mechanisms to exclude certain populations from certain borders in the name of protecting citizens.

Trafficking and terror are linked in most of these sectors that seek to reproduce rhetoric that divides the world into bad guys and good guys. Unfortunately, the bad guys tend to be portrayed as brown men, further disseminating racist and anti-immigrant sentiment globally. When our paradigms about human trafficking are broken and when the issues are misportrayed, discourse and policy continue to build on one another to increase challenges faced by Muslim populations in the post-9/11 world.

All four of the sectors introduced in this chapter are trying to make headway, and despite their tendency to obscure, omit, or ignore the nuances of trafficking it is still noteworthy and admirable that they are interested in tackling the challenges of human trafficking. What most of the sectors lack are the lived experience narratives that are so important in creating a more robust conversation about both human trafficking and terrorism. In order to untangle the many conflated strands of panic, and recognize structural factors such as inequality or the demands of our capitalist political economy, we can listen to narratives of people who have been involved in trafficking or terror. We can hear the stories of fishermen who migrated to make ends meet but found themselves working on a fishing boat that made them work 36 hour shifts without breaks or proper lighting in order to catch fish that was sold to P.F. Chang's, Walmart, and Costco (Skinner 2012). We can learn about domestic workers who left the Philippines through legal channels in order to support their families back home but were abused and harassed while working abroad and ultimately ended up detained. And we can listen to stories of former violent extremists (not only from one part of the world) to understand the draw of engaging in this field of activity. This may be where Silicon Valley can play a major role: using technology to make viral stories and experiences of people, connecting migrants and other persons involved in various industries through online resources, and helping migrants use technology as an empowering platform to organize, activate, and further enact social change. Furthermore, technology can be used to amass data, so that policies or narratives can be grounded in actual research as opposed to anecdotal evidence or political musings.

## DISCUSSION QUESTIONS

1. How have the terms "terrorism" and "trafficking" been collapsed into a single traffickingandterror paradigm, and what are the outcomes of this new paradigm today?
2. How is the traffickingandterror paradigm racialized?
3. How have each of the sectors introduced in this chapter contributed to the formation of the traffickingandterror paradigm? Can you think of other examples within these sectors?

# III: Interconnections, Interrogations, Investigations into the "Illicit"

There is a very fine line between an arms smuggler and an intelligence agent ...
(interview with Robert Muggah,
head of Small Arms Commission, February 2012)

In constructing the traffickingandterror discourse, a theme often repeated by scholars is that trafficking and terror are linked because both operate in the illegal or informal economy, and both rely upon what is referred to as "illicit networks" (Howard and Traughber 2007). The argument put forth by these scholars, and often within conversations in Washington, is that traffickers and terrorists (collapsed into the same category), have a vested interest in operating in the realm of the illicit, a realm that functions to undermine state authority and security. However, as the above quote reveals, what falls into the realm of the illicit is quite connected (1) to the definition of the licit, and (2) to the realm of the licit.[1]

We need to understand the paradigmatic construction of the illicit because much of the traffickingandterror discourse hinges on the assumption that trafficking and terror occupy the heart of darkness within illicit networks. Furthermore, laws and policies designed to operate in a way to privilege some, i.e., privilege women and children in seeking relief (though even these populations must ensure that their narratives fit the appropriate trafficking or victimizing script wherein they had absolutely no agency in their situations), punish others, i.e., male migrants who are often eclipsed in human rights initiatives or basic assistance. In addition to being gender biased, policies are also tinged with racial undertones—the U.S. recommendations for policies in Middle Eastern countries stress increased criminalization and project unfounded American anxieties about saving white women from brown men (Spivak 2006; Abu Lughod 2002).

Recent paradigms, discourses, and policies about illicit networks tend to bifurcate the realms of the licit and illicit. Moreover, there is a hierarchy that privileges the licit over the illicit and results in persons working in the illicit or informal economies

---

1  For a further discussion of the interconnectedness of the licit and illicit, see Atty and VonSchendel 2005.

being criminalized or defined as deviant. However, there are two central issues that this dichotomization obscures: (1) that the licit and illicit are very interconnected; and (2) laws and legality often produce illegality. In this chapter, I will problematize our conception of the illicit by analyzing the term and examining the **social construction** and stratification of illicit/licit, informal/formal, illegal/legal. Through a series of case studies, I will demonstrate how the two are closely intertwined, and how licit economies are often dependent on illicit networks and economies.

I next examine legal productions of illegality by focusing on why those involved in illicit networks prefer to utilize illicit or informal means rather than licit or formal networks. This analysis enables us to better understand the structural factors that lead individuals to become involved in various sectors of the informal economy. These structural factors allow us to untangle the presumptions that conflate all persons involved in trafficking with those involved in terrorism and vice versa. We can then turn our attention away from the "other" to question the role of the self in producing systems where targeted populations are made more vulnerable. Paradigms and legal interpretations help structure the contours of a threat to security as opposed to business as usual or governance. Discourse holds significant power in affecting and shaping our understandings of the illicit—constructing artificial categories of who benefits, who suffers the costs and who is punished within the illicit framework.

In general, discourses and responses to both the war on terror and war on trafficking have been colored by a sense of moral panic. In the post-9/11 context, the group of persons thought to be threatening the moral order of society typically implicates Muslim men from countries suspected to be breeding grounds for terrorism (and now trafficking), including but not limited to Saudi Arabia, Pakistan, Iran, Lebanon, Syria, Egypt, Algeria, and Tunisia. Moral panics often result in the persecution of individuals seen to be members of the morally threatening group. Historically, these groups have included communists, members of alternative sexual communities, and pagans. In his article, "Moral Panics and the Muslim," Bavelaar 2005 notes that in the wake of 9/11, moral panics led to false persecution of Muslims, Arabs, or those mistakenly thought to belong to these groups. Rhetoric about the war on terror, infused with a strong sense of Islamophobia, has led to a larger moral panic about the threat of Muslim men in particular.

In writing about human trafficking and sex work, many scholars have also pointed to the hysteria of moral panics leading to a conflation of all trafficking with sex work, and all sex work as being forced (Doezema, Weitzer, Davies, among others). In the traffickingandterror framework, the moral panic reaches extreme heights, painting an ominous picture of a shadowy, illegal economy comprised of Muslims and Arabs kidnapping white women and girls in order to fund their terrorist conglomerates. This framework has led to the creation of governing bodies such as the U.S. Department of Homeland Security and U.S. Immigration and Customs Enforcement, which have been charged with maintaining the laws that would prevent these illegal economies from threatening the sovereignty and well-being of the United States. But the moral panic fusing traffickingandterror is thought to be more terrifying because it castigates migrants and members of the informal economy as bad guys who need to be expelled, arrested, or worse, detained and tortured (as in Guantanamo).

## A Problem of Definitions

When discussing the illicit, the informal, or the illegal, it is important to highlight that these categories have been socially constructed, and that the parameters and contours of what is licit vs. illicit are unclear. Is a young woman babysitting the children of middle-class parents who is paid in cash—under the table—engaged in illegal activities? She is a member of the informal economy, but her activities are certainly not illegal, except insofar as the fact that neither the employer nor the employee has documented the transaction nor is claiming it for tax purposes. Is a woman who migrated from the Philippines to Dubai—perhaps without working papers—but who is employed as a nanny for an upper middle-class family engaged in illicit activities? How about the domestic worker in Rome who also has a side job in the sex industry? What we do know is that the designations "informal," "llicit," and "illegal" are loaded terms with the latter two suggesting more of a criminalization framework than the first.

When the terms "illegal" or "illicit" are invoked, an image of deviancy comes to mind. Whether the terms apply to the labor or goods involved, or the persons performing the labor or transacting the goods, a shadow economy is imagined. Persons involved in spheres of illicit networks are thought to be criminals or trying to scam the system. With this label of deviancy comes a layer of hyperlegality and hyperscrutiny. A recent example paints the picture more clearly.

Seventeen dining hall workers were fired from the staff of Pomona College in December of 2011. The claim was that they were illegal workers and that Pomona was required to fire them for fraudulent documents and illegal activity. Students and faculty staged teach-ins and protests to contest the decision. One fired worker powerfully noted that the only crime she had committed at Pomona was showing up to work every day on time for the past 25 years. This worker is not a deviant; Pomona College benefitted from her labor for years. To label her illegal is a misnomer.

To say she is engaging in illicit networks is not entirely accurate either, though she has labored informally for the college. Casting her as an illegal migrant paints a picture of a deviant person, thereby rendering the worker deserving of any fate that befalls him or her (however unjust). There is often a slippage of terms such as "illegal," "illicit," and "informal," without recognition of how loaded the terms are. It is for this reason that an examination of the interconnectedness of the formal/informal, licit/illicit, and legal/illegal spheres and economies can illuminate the continuum of experiences that structure lived reality.

## Perverse Integration—the Licit Depending on the Illicit

Current policy discourse highlights the rapidly growing global threat of illicit networks. The narrative of illicit economic globalization has produced a global moral panic based on extensive statistical claims and the exaggerated dichotomy of legal/illegal spheres. These narratives also underline the differences between strong state security and weak states cultivating nimble networks of organized crime. The U.S. National Intelligence Council projects a global future of failing states and the globalization of crime. Meanwhile, the U.S. government itself noted that the United States today is "threatened less by conquering states than we are by weak and failing ones" (U.S. government 2002, cited by Bourne 2011: 493). Yet this increased scrutiny on transnational crime in weak states often fails to recognize the states' own actions that foster conditions that reproduce illegal activities. The integration of organized crime with the formal economy creates a symbiotic relationship between illicit globalization and the state. Illicit networks can endure, proliferate, and reconfigure as a result of the polarizing discourse that fosters counterproductive policy prescriptions and a criminalization framework. State strengthening and securitization rhetoric perpetuate the image of a bureaucratic, yet maladroit state versus agile informal crime and trafficking networks.

Informal economies are very often perversely integrated (Duneier 1999; Hopper 2002) into formal economies, with the formal depending on the informal. Garcés Mascareñas (2010) uses the example of migrants in Spain and Malaysia to note that illegal migrants are necessary to define the "other" against the state, but more importantly, because they form a flexible oversupply of labor upon which the formal/legal economy rests. Theories of perverse integration and sociologist Manuel Castells' concept of the fourth world further exemplify the intertwined nature of legal and illegal processes and the symbiotic nature of the state and illicit networks. Castells holds that "the process of social exclusion and the insufficiency of remedial policies of social integration lead to a key process of perverse integration referred to as the labor force in the criminal economy" (Castells 1999: 1). Organized crime and illicit activities can simultaneously benefit members of the formal economy, making them an intrinsic part of systems in many countries. Perverse integration theorists such as Manuel Castells and Mitch Duneier note that informal or illicit economies are often intertwined with and depended upon by formal or licit economies, making them perverse (in that they are illicit but desirable) and integrated (in that formal economies depend on this labor). The dependence of the legal or formal on the informal can be best observed through three case studies: (1) the legalization of medical marijuana in California wherein legal dispensaries are now dependent upon illegal drug dealers to supply their growing demand, (2) agriculture and citrus growers in the United States who are dependent upon illegal workers, and (3) the historic dependence of New York City officials on organized crime for waste disposal.

The passage of Proposition 215 in California in 1996 legalized marijuana for medical purposes. Following this landmark decision, a series of dispensaries were created to provide marijuana exclusively for medical purposes. What these dispensaries, and indeed the entire state of California, did not anticipate, however, was the huge demand for medical marijuana that ensued following passage of Prop 215. Dispensaries were not able to meet this growing demand on their own through legal means of production and growing, and thus became dependent on the illicit network of marijuana growers and traffickers to bolster their supply. This dependence, however, hinged on a particular technological advancement in the form of a statewide website—Weedmaps.

Weedmaps provides a list of dispensaries for any given part of the state, broken down by county, and serves as a venue for both buyers and sellers of marijuana who operate in the illicit or informal sphere to connect with the formal sphere. Before long, the medical marijuana dispensaries were increasingly dependent on illegal marijuana growers—whom some would term "drug dealers"—to supply their growing demand (based on interviews with dispensary staff as well as dealers). In this way, the licit economy of medical marijuana becomes intertwined with the illicit economy of drug dealing.

A related example involves the agriculture and citrus growing industry in the United States. As Stewart Patrick has expertly noted (Patrick, personal communication, March 2012), the agriculture industry is able to circumvent certain labor codes in order to meet the high demands placed on agribusiness. To meet the growing demands while keeping costs low, the agriculture industry has relied on undocumented laborers (who some might define as "illegal immigrants"). These workers first began migrating to the United States over a century ago from Mexico and other parts of Latin America, and were incorporated into the country through the **Bracero guest worker** program (Cohen 2011). Guest worker programs such as Bracero often offer limited rights and documentation status for the citrus growers from Mexico who were instrumental in providing a flexible oversupply of labor for agriculture and food production. While the Bracero program has been under increased scrutiny by many academics, others point to the fact that it was a semi-formalized/legalized form of migration for labor (Cohen 2011; Mitchell 2011). Today, the agriculture industry depends on workers who migrate through illicit networks, presenting yet another example of how our formal economy of food production and consumption is dependent upon the informal economy of shadowed migration.

Finally, scholars seeking to define the term "perverse integration" also point to the example of government, state, or local actors relying on organized crime. A local example of this can be found in New York City, where city officials have been historically dependent on organized crime for the waste management of the city (Hopper 2002). While this relationship was fostered informally many years ago, the example remains salient. Indeed New York City officials would be hard pressed to construct a better system of waste management than that provided by informal networks of organized crime.

## Legal Productions of Illegality

State and individual geopolitical perspectives operate within the dichotomy of legal-illegal spheres and licitness-illicitness. Yet illegality itself marks a spatialized socio-political condition that often incites moral panics and crusades (DeGenova 2004: 160). States themselves define which activities are illicit, since laws precede and define criminality through their law-making and law-enforcing authority (Andreas 2011: 408–9). Illicit flows, as shaped by state definition, share several common character-istics: (1) they are unauthorized by the sending and/or receiving country; (2) they cross borders through methods of evading detection; and (3) they are also a source of conflict and tension in the arena of international politics (Andreas 2011: 406). Ironi-cally, many government policies that impose and enforce prohibitions can create more profitable conditions for illegal activity such as drug and migrant trafficking.

The reclassification of once legal transnational activities as criminal activities through new laws and more stringent border controls is one of the significant ways in which legal actions reproduce illegal growth. Today, the media, the U.S. government, policy makers, international organizations, and human rights groups highlight the rapid increase in activities such as migrant and sex trafficking, nuclear arms trade, and the drug trade; yet the expansive growth of illegal activity is less related to a higher transnational crime rate than it is to more ambitious and severe global prohibitions (Andreas 2011: 409). The disjuncture between the text of the law and its implemen-tation and effect reveals the failures of harsher tactics and restrictive policies. Even though these tactics initially appear to disrupt trafficking and illicit trade across bor-ders, the increase in prohibitions and criminalization can create greater benefits for illegal actors (Vance 2011: 934).

In fact, since the early 1990s migrant trafficking has become even more sophis-ticated and organized precisely because of the state's strengthening tactics. Efforts at policing do not eliminate illegality but play a role in market regulation since the method, intensity and focus of law enforcement directly reconfigures the location and form of the illegal activity, as well as size and structure of criminal organizations, and the cost and profitability of their activity (Andreas 2011: 410–11). Simply put, policies and laws to prevent trafficking are resulting in populations becoming *more* reliant on informal nodes of migration, making them more vulnerable to human trafficking (see examples in the next chapter). Similarly, UN peace operations which attempt to deter criminal networks and illicit trade can lead to increased activity within these networks and undermine the law (Holt and Boucher 2009: 24). Both the United States and international forces are unsuccessful in their efforts to stem illegal activity through increased criminalization and national security rhetoric.

The overwrought discourse labels weak states as hotbeds of sex trafficking, dangerous criminal organizations, and terrorists, which must be contained, controlled, and diverged away from state borders. Indeed, this melodrama obscures the state's own responsibility and even complicity in creating conditions favorable to trafficking (Vance 2011: 941). U.S. government releases like the *Trafficking in Persons Report* and *the International Narcotics Control Strategy Report* (n.d.), as well as government issued aggregate statistics, make bold assertions based on less than reliable data gathered from hazy methodology. The inconsistency of these reports and statistics over time and across sectors of the industry are highly problematic, yet mostly unchallenged. Economist Peter Reuter points out that the annual *International Narcotics Control Strategy Report* shows "inexplicable inconsistency over time and across sectors of the industry … some numbers are simply implausible," while another economist, the senior drug policy consultant for the UN, Francisco Thoumi, corroborates that the UN's statistics on the drug trade are equally suspect (Andreas 2011: 407). This exaggerated discourse leads to further securitization and militarization of policing efforts and unintended effects of continued illicit flows. Even though much policy discourse aims to challenge illicit flows through and within state-building processes (Ghani and Lockhart 2008, as cited by Bourne 2011), the aims of state building, counter-terrorism, and counter-narcotics are riddled with significant contradictions (Felbab-Brown 2005; Goodhand 2008, as cited by Bourne 2011: 494). The state often pursues combative measures without addressing the systemic factors that produced illegality initially. For example, the limited focus on the supply side of human trafficking and the narcotics trade concentrates the adjustment costs of increased restrictions onto marginalized groups at home and weaker states abroad (Friman 2010: 16, as cited by Bourne 2011: 494). Furthermore, the reduction or generalization of illegal actors as networks depicted as opponents of the state and engaged in "netwar" perpetuates the divisions of illegal and legal geopolitical imaginings and an equally polarized policy practice that fosters illegal activity (Arquilla and Ronfeldt 2001, as cited by Bourne 2011: 495).

The phenomenon of legality fostering illegality is a series of interconnections, not a demarcation between domestic/foreign processes or states/sprawling illicit networks. According to Andreas, "in the murky world of covert operations, the distinction between state actors and non-state illicit actors can become blurry" (2011: 417). A closer examination of the web of illegal and legal processes involved in drug, human, and arms trafficking disproves the common discourse opposing the state: a "lumbering beast and an efficient missile … unwilling and unable to change the conditions it creates and that favor transnational trafficking" (Vance 2011: 942) (including the fluid networks of organized crime, which are diverse, flexible, and barely visible). Thinking back to the socio-political spatialization of illicitness, it is important to break down the rigid distinctions between structure and actor in order to question the formation, reproduction, durability and spatiality of these various phenomena. Bourne suggests a "geopolitical imagination" as a more apt description of the interplay between networks, in which nodes in a network function as spots for the organization and transmission of illicit flows (2011: 490, 497).

The most salient production of illegality through legal prohibitions, human rights efforts, sensationalized discourse, and domestic and international policy is the issue of human trafficking. When countries tighten borders and immigration laws (as a result of the trafficking discourse which focuses hyperscrutiny on the image of the criminalized migrant), the number of people migrating through illegal and informal channels increases (Mahdavi 2011: 134). Most laws that target trafficking do not increase job opportunities at home but rather increase vulnerability of migrants who choose illegal and unregulated means. The *Trafficking in Persons Report* issued annually by the United States emphasizes increasing law enforcement, tightening borders, and raising the number of raids and arrests of trafficking offenders; however, these methods can have negative repercussions and perpetuate the arrests and criminalization of workers perceived to be illegal rather than fostering effective government initiatives (Mahdavi 2011: 203). Another way in which legal activity shapes illegal networks is evident through the influence of extra-state demands, such as NGOs, media "swarms," and pressure groups which greatly influence the state and its actions (Vance 2011: 934). The drafting, implementation as well as understanding of laws are multivalent as a result of the range of pressures from these constituencies (Shore, Write, and Pero 2011; Parnell 2003; Nader 2003; as cited by Vance 2011: 934). Human rights rhetoric of victimhood versus villains, despite its well intentions, can obscure the state's responsibility for creating the conditions that foster trafficking (Vance 2011: 942). As a result, the state responds with reactionary laws and policies that are ineffective. These inexpedient policies become especially problematic in terms of human trafficking, since it is framed as a human rights issue yet attacked through criminal law, subsequently inhibiting trafficked persons from obtaining access to protections and services.

In terms of the drug trade, much of the illegal trafficking fostered by legal practice involves cocaine and heroin. The illicit supply chains of these drugs are not just tied to local government officials; rather, foreign state actors such as intelligence agencies are central to their existence (Bourne 2011: 503). Legal focus on issues of cocaine and heroin smuggling emphasizes their connections to weak states, because of the long histories of the growth of illicit economies, prohibition regimes, and transnational influence. In the arms trade, state complicity is highly evident in nuclear smuggling (Andreas 2011: 416). Thus states can encourage illicit activity both intentionally through covert support and unintentionally through ineffective and stringent laws that reshape the market for illegal commodities. The distribution of prohibited commodities is not the only form of illicit smuggling; the smuggling of legitimate commodities is also a form of illegality created by legality. In order to evade taxes and circumvent embargoes, people will smuggle commodities such as cigarettes to generate a profit (Andreas 2011:

406). Thus international interventions in the forms of imposing economic sanctions and arms embargoes, delivering humanitarian aid, and deploying peacekeepers can exacerbate the problem of illicit networks (Andreas 2011: 421).

If the implementation of current legal practices not only fails to combat illicit networks, but unintentionally fosters their endurance, proliferation, and reconfiguration, how should global policies respond to the prevalence of illicit economic globalization? The huge disparity between policy/discourse and the lived experience of migration, forced labor and trafficking reveals the need for a departure from the criminalization framework of current policies (Mahdavi 2011: 1). International law lags in its ability to address systemic forms of criminality through prosecution and criminalization (Rothe and Collins 2011: 26). As Nollkaemper explains, "if the goal is termination of the crimes and prevention of their recurrence, individual [or singular organizations'] responsibility is unlikely to do the job" and international law should address the system that is ever revolving with replacement actors (cited in Rothe and Collins 2001: 26). In order to break from the cycle of legal intervention fostering illegal activity, government initiatives would be better directed towards reforming labor laws, restructuring the system, and strengthening civil society (Mahdavi 2011: 135).

## The Draw of the Illicit

What is most often obscured in the division between the licit and illicit is the sheer draw of illicit networks for individuals, groups, and the states that rely on these networks. Most importantly, technology has facilitated illicit networks, made anonymity more appealing and plausible, and played a major role in incentivizing the illicit over the licit. Across illicit networks, one of the most common themes that individuals and experts articulate is the somewhat perverse factor that illicit networks seem easier, more lucrative, and can expedite the flow of capital; these appealing qualities tip the balance of risk calculation in favor of the illicit. Here I provide three examples of illicit networks that present more appeal than their licit counterparts.

Anthropologist Philippe Bourgois has chronicled the lives of crack dealers in East Harlem in the 1990s in his richly detailed ethnography, *In Search of Respect: Selling Crack in El Barrio* (Bourgois 1996). In his ethnography, Bourgois depicts the structural forces at play that collide to make the illicit economy of selling drugs more appealing for this population of men. He notes that many of the men he lived with in East Harlem began dealing crack when the factories that had previously employed them shut down and moved overseas in search of lower overhead costs. Most of the employees of these factories had dropped out of high school in order to support their families. When the factories closed down, they were left without employment, but also had not attained the necessary level of education to seek other jobs.

The closure of the factories coincided with the rise of the crack epidemic in cities like Manhattan. For these men, dealing crack cocaine became the only profitable means of income generation due to their lack of education, social capital, or skill sets that would make them sought after in the formal employment sphere. His interviewees also articulated that involvement in the illicit network of drug dealing was much more desirable because they were able to make large sums of money relatively quickly. One interviewee noted that he would have to work a 12-hour shift at McDonald's (the only other employment available to him given his lack of education or job skills) to make the same amount of money he could make in 15 minutes of selling crack. As Peter Andreas notes, the advent of technology has also made drug dealing not only more profitable, but less violent. Dealers can find customers and other dealers online, and through the use of cell phones many of the face-to-face skirmishes can be avoided. With the decrease in risk of violence, the appeal of this illicit network becomes even higher (personal communication, April 2012).

Another group of persons for whom illicit networks can hold more draw are migrants, and in particular, female migrants. With the passage of anti-trafficking laws in line with recommendations found in the U.S. *Trafficking in Persons Report*, many countries have rushed to tighten borders to prevent female migrants in particular from leaving their homes. Examples of these laws include the **Philippine Household Service Reform Package** of 2006, as well as a recent law passed in Ethiopia,[2] both of which state that women under the age of 30 and unmarried women should be discouraged from migrating abroad. The problem with these policies is that women still need to migrate to make ends meet. When these laws are passed, female migrants must rely on illicit networks to facilitate their journeys to countries with employment opportunities that can ensure their families' livelihoods.

Other female migrants in sending countries such as Nigeria and Eritrea noted that they preferred to avail themselves of illicit migratory networks because they trusted them more than official routes through their own Ministries of Labor. An Eritrean woman who was working in Dubai when I met her indicated that it would take too long to migrate legally, thus the illegal route of smuggling would give her access to capital more quickly. Similar to drug dealing, technology has facilitated illicit networks, thereby increasing their draw as risk is minimized. Many of the migrant women I met while conducting field work in Dubai noted that they found their recruiters (what some may call smugglers) through online services, making the ability to find and tap into illicit networks that much easier.

Finally, the sex industry is also an illicit network that holds much appeal; female laborers indicate that the advent of technology has increased the draw of this informal

---

2 For more information about this legislature, see http://www.protectionproject.org/wp-content/uploads/2010/09/Ethiopia_Criminal-Code-TIP_2004.pdf or pages 58–66 of http://www.ilo.org/public/english/region/afpro/addisababa/sro/pdf/ilotipethiopia.pdf. See also http://ilo-mirror.library.cornell.edu/public/english/region/afpro/addisababa/publ/femalemigrants.pdf

economy as risk decreases. Many sex workers now advertise, screen, and connect with clients online, making dangerous street-based sex work less necessary. According to Jessie Nicole, director of the Sex Workers Outreach Project in Los Angeles, sex workers depend on the Internet as a safe way of engaging in this form of illicit networks, because they feel safer from law enforcement, no longer need pimps or brokers, and can share information with one another about clients and dangers quickly (interview, March 10, 2012). Furthermore, technology has been used to provide anonymous STD and HIV testing, with results disseminated to client bases and other sex workers, and also to increase availability of education and prevention resources. With the decrease in risk and increase in resources that technology provides, many women report finding the illicit economy of sex work more appealing given the speed of income generation and other opportunities it provides.

Disentangling the interconnections between the licit/illicit, legal/illegal, and formal/informal reveals the socially constructed nature of moral panics that focus on particular crimes within particular populations. The traffickingandterror moral panic has recently manifested the fear of illicit networks undermining the sovereignty and safety of legal/licit spaces. The paradigm has constructed an image of a particular bad guy, without recognizing the structural context that leads individuals to engage in questionable activities; and as a result, many persons involved in various aspects of the informal economy find themselves caught in the net that is cast wide enough to capture and combat the threats posed by the illicit networks of traffickingandterror. This net functions simultaneously to (1) further reify the terrifying Muslim (Rana 2011) trope, (2) collapse anyone involved in terrorism or trafficking into the same frame, and (3) provide a framework wherein all persons involved in illicit networks could be arrested and punished as being threats and opponents in both the wars on terror and trafficking. The operationalization and codification of laws hinges on interpretation and enforcement, emboldening the shades of gray that color the legal-illegal spectrum. An analysis of who gets punished, how, and how often can illuminate the contours of discourse surrounding this topic, and can illustrate how the wars on terror and trafficking are fought both locally and globally on a daily basis. In the next section, I show how the hyperfocus of law enforcement demonstrates the particular interpretations of laws, and reveals the power of the traffickingandterror paradigm in framing actions taken against migrants of particular racial and religious origins. This hyperfocus also shows how the traffickingandterror frame has conveniently turned an anti-immigration campaign into one of protection of citizens.

## Hyperfocus, Hyperlegality

Government policy and the scope and level of its law enforcement struggle to effectively target illicit networks because the extent, definitions, and contours of them vary based upon the influence of moral panics. States can pursue a war on trafficking in limited ways that fail to address the systemic factors that produce and shape illicit networks (Bourne 2011: 494). Significant focus is placed on individual processes, rather than acknowledging the complex combinations of the macro and micro processes involved. State security discourse emphasizes rigid distinctions between structure and actor, and constructs illicit networks as hierarchical and threatening; however, an investigation of the formation, reproduction, durability, and spatiality of networks reveals that they are horizontal rather than a vertical or hierarchical integration of assorted nodes (Bourne 2011: 497). Illicit networks are interspersed and interconnected; yet laws and policies concentrate on individual criminal networks and fail to acknowledge this entangled nature of state and non-state actors. These limited forms of policy prescriptions detach states, especially first world powers, from any responsibility. The level of enforcement needs to be more broadly focused and recognize that the **commodity chains** of illicit networks are not linear but rather a series of murky webs that cannot be eliminated merely through specified and criminalized targets.

Illicit markets involve the distribution of products through a commodity chain, which is comprised of several links: source (production and smuggling), supply, sales, and feeders (finance and parasite behavior) (Malm, Kinney, and Pollard 2008: 273). Multiple interconnections are apparent between individuals involved in certain source niches such as production, smuggling and transportation with suppliers and with retailers, yet law enforcement that targets specific individuals often fails to eliminate the targeted activity. Specific foci of law enforcement obscure the complexities of involvement and also fail to recognize that the "the method, intensity and focus of law enforcement can profoundly shape the location and form of smuggling, the size and structure of smuggling organizations and cost and profitability" (Andreas 2011: 410).

Throughout various levels of enforcement, states are not deemed responsible or complicit in the existence of illicit networks; international crimes are attributed to individuals not the state or organizations (Boussiouni, 2010a, as cited by Rothe and Collins, 2011: 26). The state targets specific actors who have evidence of engaging in illegal activities, however, because perversely integrated structures of illicit networks have ever-revolving actors, they continue to thrive. This complex web of actors, with varying degrees of complicity and accountability amongst individuals, organizations (from corporations to states), and networks of organized syndicates (Rothe and Collins, 2011: 24) is largely ignored in anti-trafficking rhetoric and policy. Actors are essentialized as "'networks,' which are viewed as opponents of the state and engaged in netwar" (Arquilla and Ronfeldt 2001, as cited by Bourne 2011: 496). By demonizing non-state actors specifically through criminality, the narrow-focused laws and policies are both ineffective and reactionary.

The Palermo Protocol (UN 2000) casts trafficking as part of international criminal conspiracies through its definition of an "organized criminal group" as three or more people acting together (UN Protocol, Article 4, following the definition provided by the Convention against Transnational Organized Crime, Article 2, as cited by Vance 2011). Thus, law enforcement focuses on policing, securitizing and militarizing, as well as targeting individuals rather than acknowledging the necessity of effecting more systemic change. As Vance states, "the prospect of effectively applying criminal law and sanctions to these multitudes of small-scale networks deeply embedded in communities is unpromising" (938).

The hyperfocus on criminalization not only fails to fragment illicit networks, but also fails to protect trafficked persons whose rights can be compromised or violated. According to a Congressional report from 2010, the U.S. focuses on both "assistance to victims of trafficking" and "law enforcement efforts to arrest and prosecute traffickers" (Siskin and Wyler 2010: 15 ). However, trafficked persons who are noncitizens and illegal immigrants are often prevented from seeking help and their ability to provide testimony during a criminal trial is compromised. More specifically, the provision of a T-visa, a trafficking visa intended to assist and permit the survivor to remain in the United States, is predicated upon the survivor's willingness to testify against his or her trafficker. If the trafficker is (1) not known to him or her, (2) a member of his or her family, or (3) has threatened harm to his or her family back home, the survivor is not likely to testify against this person or group of people, being rendered vulnerable and without access to a T-visa. Both the United States and international laws against trafficking are criminal codes, and while the criminal prosecution of traffickers may be necessary, the current framework does not allow for trafficked persons to claim human rights protections or access services. As Vance explains, "the emphasis makes it difficult for trafficked people to escape the vortex that deems them criminal offenders, even in texts that nod to their new (but in most countries optional) status as crime victims" (2011: 936). The fact that anti-trafficking laws are placed within the UN's Office of Drugs and Crime obscures the sometimes beneficial role of transnational crime activities for some members of the community; the hyperfocused criminalization framework does not allow for the recognition that transnational crime activities can actually be viewed as legitimate employment opportunities by some members of the population, frequently those who are marginalized and unable to successfully integrate with the legal economy.

In addition to this focus on specific actors and the tendency to criminalize trafficked persons as well as traffickers, law enforcement is also limited in its treatment of failed and weak states as the hotbeds of illicit activity. Trafficking and other illicit networks are treated as linear processes that move danger one way from failed states outwards (Bourne 2011: 493). Both domestic and international policy circles assume direct links between weak states and transnational threats, which has become a "conventional wisdom" central to the logic of much western security practice (Patrick 2006: 29, as cited in Bourne 2011: 491). Furthermore, current anti-trafficking discourse and security practice tends to attribute underlying causes of trafficking to an "amorphous 'poverty'" (Vance 2011). This scrutiny on weak and failed states rather than a recognition of interconnections amongst numerous states can result in counterproductive policy prescriptions such as calls to further securitize and militarize policing efforts (Andreas 2011: 423). Law enforcement and security practice often focus on a limited range of supply side factors, which results in a shift of adjustment costs of prohibitions onto marginal groups at home and weaker states abroad (Friman 2010: 16, as cited in Bourne 2011: 494). Interdiction efforts by the U.S. military and law enforcement agencies against transport and concealment of products from the developing world forces traffickers and cartels to develop "ever more ingenious evasion techniques and less obvious, if more convoluted routes" (Williams and Brown 2012: 422) and does not successfully dismantle these criminal networks.

Even though the above methods of state hyperfocus are rooted in statistical evidence, the lack of hard data makes it much more challenging for governments to structure effective and realistic responses. The UN Office on Drugs and Crime provides estimates of the scope of various illicit networks, however, these figures (and all trafficking network figures) can be politicized and are founded on assumptions and guesswork. The U.S. Department of State estimates that roughly 800,000 people are trafficked across borders each year, and if trafficking within countries is included in these total figures, some two to four million people are trafficked annually juxtapose this with the number of 27 million trafficked persons globally used by internationally acclaimed NGO Free the Slaves and Kevin Bales. These numbers typically go unchallenged, even though they are most likely overestimates.

The exorbitantly high volume of sex trafficking literature, media discourse, and statistical analysis indicates a biased focus on sex trafficking rather than other forms of illicit networks. There is a specific focus on women and children, which lends itself to policies that ignore other migrants and laborers, such as male construction worker migrants who face equally if not more abusive and degrading situations without any recourse. The "saving" rhetoric entrenched in anti-sex trafficking campaigns results in brothel raids, detention, and deportation, which do not allow sex workers other avenues for aid within their industry but rather castigates all sex workers as victims. Meanwhile, male migrants and trafficked persons unengaged in sex work are largely ignored.

The U.S. State Department inextricably links prostitution with force and coercion and casts it as an illegitimate form of labor with its rhetoric from the 2008 TIP Report to Congress. The report states that "sex trafficking would not exist without the demand for commercial sex flourishing around the world" and that prostitution "should not be regulated as a legitimate form of work for any human being" (Siskin and Wyler 2010: 38). Even though some argue that U.S. government anti-trafficking efforts have a bias, which disproportionately focuses on sex trafficking and that a higher percentage of the anti-trafficking budget is allocated to NGOs who seek to rescue women and children from the sex industry, a Congressional report from 2010 counters that "inventories of U.S. anti-trafficking programs since 2004 appear to counter these claims as they show U.S. support for a wide variety of NGOs that strive to protect victims and prosecute traffickers engaged in all types of human trafficking (Siskin and Wyler 2010: 37). However, since the Trafficking Victims Protection Reauthorization Act of 2003 (P.L. 108–193) restricts government funding to be given only to groups that oppose prostitution (Siskin and Wyler 2010: 37), the United States is focusing not only on anti-sex trafficking groups as the only groups requiring aid, but specifically on anti-sex trafficking with an agenda to abolish prostitution.

There is a disjuncture between the U.S. government's belief in its broad-based focus on all forms of trafficking and the criticism of international groups and governments and groups external to the government; frequently the state apparatus fails to recognize how its focused initiatives obscure the complexities of trafficking and other illicit networks. U.S. policy prescriptions are also at odds with those of the UN and other international forms of governance. At the same time that the United States has a tendency to concentrate its relief efforts on victims of prostitution and trafficked women and children, the UN Palermo Protocol (2000) has expanded its definition in trafficking to include that trafficking "victimizes children, women and men (not just women, or adults, but also men and children)" and "is for a range of exploitative purposes (not just sexual exploitation)" (United Nations Office on Drugs and Crime). This marks a significant departure from the UN's General Assembly's Protocol to Prevent, Suppress and Punish Trafficking in Persons, Especially Women and Children in 2000, which clearly delineated trafficking as a feminized and sexualized issue. Even though there has been some progress with the UN and the U.S. government recognizing all trafficking, not just the trafficking of sex workers, the discourse surrounding all illicit networks and security policies is still fraught with issues of hyperfocusing and obscuring connections.

Illicit networks overlap and are perversely integrated into the economy, while law enforcements are unidirectional and hyperfocused on individual aspects and on specific illicit networks of sex trafficking. Individual actors, micro processes, and weak states are still targeted in a criminalized framework, and state policies do not recognize the need for a multi-pronged approach. The state needs to take a broader focus on the structural violence and the forms of systemic exclusion it perpetuates that fuel involvement in transnational criminal activities. A more holistic and human rights framework approach would include a delivery of basic services, rather than a hyperfocus on tightening borders and criminalizing specific actors, which further push illicit networks underground and into the margins where they are less likely to be regulated or resolved.

## DISCUSSION QUESTIONS

1. How are the informal, illegal, and illicit economies social constructs?
2. What are some examples of the legal/licit depending on the illegal/illicit outside of what has been presented in this chapter?
3. How do presumed links between weak states and organized crime obscure larger macro-social challenges?

# IV: Living the Wars on Terror and Trafficking

My life in Dubai was not great, but it was not terrible. I was getting by. And then it happened. They came for me, just one night as I was walking home. They came for me. Then they sent me home. I never understood what happened.

> (Ethiopian domestic worker who was rounded up on an anti-trafficking rescue mission and forcibly deported, 2009)

When the Philippines government made rules to protect us, rules that said we shouldn't go abroad to work unless we had training, unless the employers had agreed to a lot of things, they just closed the door, but opened the window. Lots more migrants went illegally because they couldn't go through the government. That made them illegal.

> (Domestic workers' rights activist in Manilla, 2010)

Being Pakistani, I was a second-class citizen growing up in the Gulf. I worked hard though, and I managed to get into college in the U.S. and did well. Then 9/11 happened, and I became a second-class citizen in the U.S. I was suddenly unwelcome at my job, my apartment, everywhere. I was sent home to a home I didn't know. They sent me to Islamabad. Yes, that's where I'm a citizen of, but I don't know Islamabad. Now I must learn a new city, a new way of life.

> (Pakistani engineer living in Islamabad, 2011)

I don't think you should ask how we want to be rescued. You should ask "what causes that reality?" Because if you rescue one of us, there will be another person to take our place immediately. Who replaces us? Rather than rescue, we need to eliminate the conditions that make it possible for slavery to exist. It's not just about escape or rescue, it's about taking a stand.

> (Mexican agricultural worker and activist in the United States, 2012)

Unfortunately, many of the deeply flawed but well-intentioned saving and rescue paradigms that have emerged from the wars on terror and trafficking are undergirded by a racialized morality. This form of morality inadvertently reinforces distinctions between white saviors and the minorities who require their help and interference. Even though many involved in the war on trafficking or in the war on terror seek to improve the lives of migrants who are trafficked in the Middle East or seek to liberate women who are caught in structures we don't fully comprehend, the mere fact that they are instigating changes for the "other" reinforces issues of racism and sexism and condemns the "other" to a perpetually low and helpless status. In all of the discourses surrounding trafficking, terror, and traffickingandterror, a "saving" rhetoric emerges that (1) reinforces both a division and a hierarchy between us and them (where we need to go and save them often from themselves), (2) presumes that all persons in a particular part of the world or in particular industries need saving, (3) assumes that saving is only accomplished through rescue, detainment, deportation, or forcibly living in a rescue camp, and (4) leads to policies designed to prevent the migration of certain populations into certain borders. This misappropriated saving denies the agency of the populations in need of better options, rather than control and forced rescue missions, and leads to increased policing, increased criminalization, and reinforced structural violence. These new policies tinged with racialized morality are manifested in anti-immigration measures that can cause more persons to rely on informal means of migration (which can often be more exploitative).

In this chapter, I will draw on ethnographic data, field research, and interviews to compare the lived experience with paradigms, policies, and rescue rhetoric. The traffickingandterror paradigm has resulted in widespread campaigns to save certain women of color while keeping out Muslim men. I highlight the adverse impact of saving discourses: the policies and outreach strategies fomented by the construction of certain persons as victims and others as villains. The focus of the chapter is on the experiences of individuals who are in difficult situations because of the traffickingandterror frame, and who find their challenges compounded by policies or outreach strategies that seek to restrict their rights. Through the narratives of two men who were deported after suffering forced labor for many years, I show the repercussions of misplaced rescue efforts and what life after trafficking is like for many individuals. Contrary to popular paradigms, life after trafficking can often be worse for many individuals because structural changes need to take place to eliminate the conditions that make forced labor, deportation, and racialized policies a reality.

## Rescue Gone Wrong

"I never knew what hit me," said Layla, a 27-year-old Iranian woman who had been working in the sex industry throughout various parts of the Gulf but was living on the streets of Tehran when I met her in 2007. A slender woman with long black hair that she struggled to tuck under a veil, she had started working in Dubai in 2005 as an income generating strategy to support her daughter and parents back in Tehran. "They never knew what I did in Dubai, or later Kuwait or Qatar. They thought I was a businesswoman, which I am. But me traveling here to do my work kept me safe. I could make a lot of money, and no one had to know where the money was coming from. The important thing was that I was making money and my parents could eat. That was all," Layla explained. After her husband left her and her parents fell ill, Layla could not find viable alternatives to support her family. She tried working in homes as a caregiver and domestic worker, but the pay was inconsistent. When she heard about work in the sex industry, she said she jumped at the opportunity, reasoning that work as a high-end escort was "easier than scrubbing toilets or changing diapers," and the pay was rumored to be much higher.

Layla moved between various cities in the Gulf because she felt it was easier to avoid the authorities if she didn't stay in one place for too long. After working for several weeks/months in Dubai, Doha, and Riyadh, she heard there was a high-end brothel in Abu Dhabi where women could contract their own clients and rent safe space. Like many of the other sex workers I interviewed throughout my fieldwork in Tehran and Dubai, Layla never had a pimp or broker but rather handled her clientele herself. When it came to safety concerns, she relied on informal networks of other sex workers to screen clients and identify safe spaces. "One of my most trusted friends told me about the Abu Dhabi brothel," Layla recalled. "She said it was a safe, clean space, and that the clients were kind. And she was right. When I arrived in Abu Dhabi, I saw that it was exactly as she described. Like a heaven for sex workers!" she said laughing. But Layla's luck did not last long. Two weeks after she arrived in Abu Dhabi, the U.S.-based TIP report was released, giving the UAE a low ranking on the Tier 2 watch list. The TIP recommended that the UAE increase prosecutions of sex trafficking and ramp up their rescue operations. Three weeks later, the brothel Layla was working at was raided, and all of the women were taken into custody and detained.

"They [the police] said they were coming to help us. To save us, they said. But they hit us, treated us like animals. One of them grabbed me by my hair and threw me in the truck. My friend Laudan was taken in the back and raped by another officer. We didn't understand what was happening. Then they sent us to jail," Layla recalled, her eyes swelling with tears. After three days in jail, a social worker came to see Layla and her friends. "This lady kept saying she was there to help, that she was going to help us all go home. But we didn't want to go home, we wanted to stay in Abu Dhabi and keep working." Layla's sentiments echo what many other women have narrated: a desire to remain in the host country, even if working conditions are not ideal. "What people don't realize is that home isn't always a good place, not a place we want to go to," said one Polish woman who was working in the informal economy selling beauty products in Dubai. "Yes, I'm illegal here, yes, a lot of things go wrong, but if I go home, it will be worse. For some of us, home means death," said an Ethiopian woman who had been arrested on a raid mission in Dubai but managed to escape.

The social worker and police officers told the women that they could stay in the UAE if they were willing to testify against their traffickers. "But I didn't have a trafficker, I didn't even know what that was," Layla remembered. "So, they beat me. They said they would beat his name out of me. They asked me who my pimp was, I said I didn't have one, so they beat me again." They told her she was not eligible for residence in the local women's shelter and would receive no protection because she was uncooperative and did not testify against her trafficker. After four weeks of unrelenting questioning and abuse, Layla was deported back to Iran. Her rescue involved a brothel raid and misplaced attempts to help through the use of police enforcement and punishing the trafficking rather than assisting Layla with a shelter or other protections. Upon returning to Iran, it was revealed that she had been engaging in sex work for two years. Furious, her father began beating her and eventually broke one of her legs. He then kicked her out of the house and forbid her from ever seeing her daughter or family again. Unable to walk and weakened from all that she had endured during the rescue mission, Layla was relegated to living on the streets, sometimes using drugs to ease the pain, and begging for food just to survive.

Sadly, Layla is not the only person suffering the adverse effects of rescue campaigns. Numerous cases and studies reveal how rescue, the most common response deployed in the war on trafficking, can feel more oppressive than the working conditions under which many women and men earn their livelihood. For instance, Elena Shih, who works with trafficking survivors in China and Thailand, noted that many of the rescue organizations are faith based and strongly encourage the survivors they rescue to convert to Christianity and attend mandatory church services daily and added that many rehabilitation programs also restrict the movement of the survivors, making many of them feel more trapped than when they were working in conditions of force, fraud, or coercion. Shih recounted the story of a Thai woman who explained that she felt more free as a sex worker than she did living in the rehabilitation program where she was forced to attend church, banned from leaving the compound, or seeing any of her old friends and colleagues, and while working to make jewelry with very little pay (Shih personal communication, February 2012). Ann Jordan, a long time human trafficking advocate and the director of Rightswatch, an international trafficking research organization, echoed some of Shih's concerns. At a roundtable on the theme of "Rescue Gone Wrong" held in Google's Mountain View Campus on May 27, 2012, Jordan corroborated that similar problems even arise amidst large-scale rescue operations such as the highly funded and much heralded International Justice Mission. Jordan indicated that in a study of survivors of human trafficking who had been rescued by the International Justice Mission in Nepal, within 12 months of their rescue, 70 percent had converted to Christianity (Jordan 2012). Other participants on the roundtable remarked that many of the rescue campaigns are lacking sustainable solutions. After survivors are rescued, they are either held in rehabilitation programs (which many wish to be released from) or they are deported with the assumption that home is a better place (or a better and safer environment). At least half of the women I interviewed in Dubai who were deported to countries such as Iran, Ethopia, Russia, Poland, and Pakistan reported far worse conditions when arriving home, similar to Layla's experience.

In their groundbreaking edited volume, *The Deportation Regime* (2010), Nicholas DeGenova and Natalie Peutz and show how deportation is socially constructed and normalized as an operation tangential to the workings of a global regime. They explain that deportation is typically something we categorize as a natural and intrinsic part of state sovereignty; however, this classification of deportation is a construct that is socially produced and rooted in our society and our time. Deportation is not an ahistorical and inherent form of forced departure across state lines despite its normalization in our everyday vernacular; rather, it is a violation of rights. The reified category of deportation hinges on the constructed category of states and state boundaries which are similarly viewed as natural and timeless when in fact they, too, are a social product. The social production of deportation as a regime is not only created and reinforced between sending and receiving states, but is also a consistent part of the global discourse. Since deportability is now substituted as an innate manifestation of state control as well as state sovereignty, it is important to look at the social ramifications. The status of deportability goes unquestioned in the global discourse and commonly links deportable laborers to a state of illegality and even sub-humanness, creating inevitable and harmful forms of social discipline and labor subordination. Unfortunately, in many instances, rescue has become code for deportation, where rescue maintains positive and helpful connotations to its more menacing deportation counterpart. But while they conjure different socially constructed methods of saving or punishing, rescue and deportation are often one and the same. Many rescue strategies are premised on the notion that migrants wish to go home, that home is a clear cut place, or that home is a better option for them than their current situation.

When discussing the notion of rescue, Sienna Baskin, a senior strategist at the Urban Justice Center, emphasizes, "most women, if they actually want to get out, rescue themselves." The notion that all sex workers need or want rescue is false (Bernstein 2007; Coalition Against Trafficking in Women [CATW], Sex Worker's Outreach Project [SWOP]). The idea that many migrants who are in situations of forced labor are awaiting rescue is also false. Most of the migrants with whom I have spoken around the world during my research indicated that they are working to get *themselves* out of their current situations. Unfortunately, much of the saving and rescue rhetoric ignores migrants' ability to take action and determine their own path away from forced labor, or even sex workers' ability to choose to continue their line of work. As a result, the saving and rescue rhetoric can be condescending and remove or deny agency.

The premise that people, especially in certain parts of the world or in certain industries require "saving" more than others (most often women, women of color, and/or women in the sex industry), also presupposes a racialized power imbalance and a flawed developmentalist framework. Not only do some people not want to be rescued, but many find the experience of outside rescue operations frightening or abusive. Still others note that migrants should be empowered to work towards their own goals, which for some migrants does include getting out of the challenging situations they are in and returning home, but for others means finding shelters or healthcare or other assistance while continuing to live in the country they moved to or the employment they sought out. The most sustainable and far reaching solution rather than just rescue operations (which if anything perpetuate the vicious cycle of trafficking), would be to address the conditions that cause people to seek out illegal/informal avenues of migration and employment. As "G," who is quoted at the beginning of this chapter, noted, more important than rescue is working to change the structural conditions that cause systems of inequality. One of the most powerful avenues we have to change structure is policy. Sadly, however, because many of our policies are not in line with lived experience, they are not only *not* changing the structural barriers, but increasing the challenges that many face.

## Policies Gone Wrong

"What does it matter if I was trafficked or not?" asked Abeba, an Ethiopian woman standing in line at the Ethiopian embassy in Dubai. Abeba had left her home in Addis Ababa when her father took up with another woman, leaving her mother and her three sisters without any source of income and saddled with large debts. After hearing about the abundance of work for women in the Gulf, Abeba sought out employment abroad through the Ministry of Labor. When she arrived, however, a ministry official told her that she would not be able to secure employment abroad for some time. "He said because they were concerned about trafficking, and that they didn't want to let single women leave, he said for this I cannot go," she recalled, reflecting on a recent policy enacted by the Ethiopian government in response to the TIP report which suggested that trafficking could be diminished by restricting the out migration of single women, or women under the age of 30. But Abeba, like many others I met, needed to leave immediately, and she needed to find employment so that she could support her family, which led her to contract with a local broker to work as a hotel maid in one of Dubai's newest and largest hotels.

When Abeba arrived, she was made to work long hours, and often didn't see a single paycheck for months on end. On more than one occasion, she was sexually harassed by the hotel clientele who assumed she was available to them based on the fact that, as she explained, "I was a woman, I was dark skinned and I was in their room." One night a hotel guest raped her and then stuffed 200 dirhams ($50 USD) into her uniform pocket before leaving. "I'm not sure why people think that all Ethiopian women are prostitutes and should be locked up," Abeba explained, referring to the fact that when she went to the police to complain, they assumed she was a sex worker and arrested her on the spot. She spent three weeks in jail before one of her managers came to bail her out.

Not wanting to return to her old job, Abeba went to the Ethiopian Embassy for assistance. The first time she visited the embassy, she was repeatedly asked if she was trafficked. When she told her story about wanting to come to Dubai, it was assumed that since she was complicit in making the decision to migrate (and was not taken as the dominant tropes of trafficking suggest), she did not fit the trafficking script, and thus perhaps was less deserving of assistance. Furthermore, she was castigated for circumventing the legal routes of migration. "They told me I was stupid to rely on a broker, and that's why this happened to me," she recalled. By the time I had met Abeba, she had already absconded from her job, was living on the streets of Dubai, and could not afford a ticket home. She was unsure what to do next and was working illegally selling stolen goods to tourists to make ends meet. In her case, the trafficking discourse had not only failed to protect her rights but had increased her challenges in migration and in the host country where she was assumed to be a criminal. Her situation, unfortunately not unique, is one of the most glaring examples of the negative repercussions of state and global discourse and policies casting people as illegal and deportable.

Some of the most obvious pitfalls of the trafficking rhetoric as espoused in policy recommendations such as the TIP, or in popular discourse such as *Taken* or *Call and Response* derive from the focus on prosecution, criminalization, and the need to fit a programmatic paradigm or script of helplessness. Though the United Nations defines trafficking as all instances of "force, fraud, or coercion" (UN Palermo Protocol 2000), the interpretation of trafficking and the operationalization of policies to "combat trafficking" focus predominantly on scripted narratives that relinquish all agency and typically involve forced labor in the sex industry.

Sama, a migrants' rights activist, who is also a migrant from Ethiopia to Dubai herself, is very articulate on this issue: "The problem is that your George Bush and the Americans made trafficking so political, just by the ways the policies are written. Look at the TVPA—it's all about sex trafficking. On top of that they made it so that all trafficking is sex trafficking, so what does that do? It makes people racist, it makes people think that any Ethiopian woman here is a sex worker, or has been trafficked, and is a criminal." Every day Sama works with Ethiopian women who have been arrested for absconding from their jobs, overstaying their visas, accruing debt, or working as sex workers. She said that the blatant and pointed focus on sex trafficking within the TIP and in United Nations documents such as the Palermo Protocol (which operates under the umbrella of the UN Office on Drugs and Crime) has constructed the trafficking issue as a criminal matter in the minds of locals and UAE law enforcement. Sama was frustrated that members of law enforcement assume that women from certain nation-alities must all be guilty.

Local and international authorities articulate and reproduce racialized and gen-dered hierarchies rather than approaching labor and migration issues within a human rights framework. Sama was also angered by international policies, such as those advo-cated in the TIP report, that consider all abused migrant women to be sex workers and, by default, criminals. Thus any migrant worker seeking assistance is first taken to jail for questioning. "The worst part is that they don't even get good translators for these women. They—the police, or the judges—they have made up their minds about Ethiopian women, and they get people to translate for them into words that they want to hear, that they are guilty, that they are criminals. They don't even get a fair shot, that's why I insist on doing the translations, because it's just not fair," she explained.

Sama pulled out a photograph from her purse. In it, a frail Ethiopian woman not weighing more than 90 pounds was lying in a hospital bed. The woman was hooked up to an IV drip, but her arms were also handcuffed to the bed. Sama continued, raising her ordinarily soft voice for the first time: "Yes, can you believe it? She is handcuffed to the bed! She ran away because her employer was abusing her, she was a housemaid. She ran away and as she was doing so she was hit by a car and was taken to the hospital. When she woke up, she was chained to the bed. They assume that because she ran away, and because she is an Ethiopian woman, she is a criminal. Now how do you handle that kind of racism?"

Her voice once again became soft as she explained that things weren't always this way; that people didn't used to be this harsh toward migrant women, and that doing her job used to be much easier. She acknowledged that there has been a long history of labor rights violations in the UAE, but stresses that in the late 1990s, migrant advocacy groups were beginning to make progress vis-à-vis the state; progress that was stunted, in her opinion, with the politicization of the trafficking issue. She emphasized that it was only when the issue became political, when the UAE was put on the TIP watch list, that female migrant workers became synonymous with sex workers and, as sex workers, became labeled as trafficking victims—seen as a dangerous, politically damaging population that demanded what some would call protection in the form of observation and surveillance.

Beyond unilateral sending country policies such as the Ethiopian policy that Abeba encountered, global policies such as the TIP report that seek to regulate the movement of (female) bodies across borders (Cheng 2010; Parrenas 2011) also have a negative impact on migrant women and on the countries subject to high levels of scrutiny. Furthermore, the TIP, with its hyperfocus on prosecution and the sex industry, has eclipsed the migrants' rights issue.

Throughout the 1990s, a movement had been building in the UAE to address the issue of migrants' rights. Groups of co-ethnics or co-workers began coming together to lobby the government for a reform of the sponsorship system that structures migrant experiences in the UAE.[1] Migrants' rights groups worked collaboratively to push for expanded labor rights and an eventual overhaul of the sponsorship system, which they argued was at the root of infringements on migrants' rights. Grassroots efforts to modify the sponsorship system had just begun to receive government attention when the war on trafficking took center stage. In 2005, the UAE was given a low ranking in the TIP report. Unlike its neighbors such as Iran, the UAE was invested in its international reputation, especially vis-à-vis one of its major trading partners, the United States. With the creation of the TIP report, a chain of events, cyclical and simultaneous at points, was put into motion. The TIP, with its focus on sex trafficking and prosecution, shifted governmental attention away from migrants' rights (the real heart of trafficking violations) to hyperscrutiny of the sex industry. Sex workers became the target of raid and rescue campaigns, and anti-trafficking initiatives from the United States started making their way into the Emirates at the level of discourse as well as action. The TIP was very clear in its directives toward the UAE:

> The United Arab Emirates (UAE) is a destination country for men and women trafficked for the purposes of labor and commercial sexual exploitation ... [G]overnment authorities continue to interpret the anti-trafficking law to exclude some who have been forced into commercial sexual exploitation of labor ... (r)ecommendations for the UAE: continue to increase law enforcement efforts to identify, prosecute and punish acts of sex trafficking ...
> (Trafficking in Persons Report on the UAE 2008: 253)

A snowball became an avalanche, escalating with its own momentum. Most importantly, perhaps, is that attention was directed away from reforming the sponsorship system and protecting migrants' rights as laborers and zeroed in on policing the sex industry specifically. This shift led to an increase in arrests and deportation of sex workers from a variety of backgrounds. A secondary result was that U.S. anti-trafficking efforts began to focus on saving the poor women in the Gulf, as one Los Angeles-based activist told me in 2008. American-backed anti-trafficking organizations such as the now infamous City of Hope[2] took on a new mandate to fight trafficking. The local Emirati response was to create a vice squadron within the police department

---

1  For more about the *kefala* or sponsorship system, see Gardner 2010; Longva, 1999, 2005; or Mahdavi 2011.

2  City of Hope was an organization founded by an American woman living in the UAE to assist women and children who experienced abuse while in the UAE. Less than a decade after the organization's founding, it was revealed that staff at City of Hope were actually abusing and trafficking women who came to them to seek assistance. For more information about this case, see http://www.uaelawdirectory.com

to focus specifically on trafficked women. These police officers, imported most often from neighboring Bangladesh or Sri Lanka, were not trained to work with sex workers or to identify trafficked persons. The result, as many sex workers articulated, was increased abuse from police officers who conducted raids in the name of rescue, but who treated sex workers as criminals not victims. In this context of heightened scrutiny of all migrant women, local activists seeking to provide services to migrant women also came under harsh evaluation from state actors now much more inclined to deny approval for their initiatives and to criminalize their actions.

In a subsequent year, one of the state department officials working on the TIP report noted that one of the recommendations was to "tighten borders," meaning to restrict the numbers of women coming into the country, a requirement blatantly at odds with the persistent demand for female labor in the Gulf and the regular supply of women looking to migrate to the region in search of employment (personal communication, October 2009). Thus, as Julia O'Connell Davidson (2006) notes, when the demand for mobility in migrant-receiving countries is coupled with restrictive immigration policies, this conjuncture of two inconsistent practices creates irregular migratory patterns that may be exploitative. In the context of the UAE, women migrating from other parts of Asia and Africa must increasingly rely on unlicensed middlemen in order to procure employment in the Gulf. This irregular path leads to illegal immigration and work status in the host country. The TIP thus perpetuates the cycle of illegality and trafficking violations as increased border controls lead to increasingly underground avenues of migration. Rather than combatting trafficking, global police initiatives such as the TIP report produce conditions of illegal migrancy.

Receiving governments are also implicated in the construction of state-produced illegality; the TIP and other global policy initiatives are not the only state entities that are complicit in the socially constructed status of being illegal. Governments of states which receive significant migrant flows foster increased conditions of force, fraud, and coercion because of their role in producing the societal conditions that generate demand for unregulated labor which as employers remark, is "cheaper, more expendable, and easier to control" (interview with construction site manager in Dubai 2008).

## Paradigms Gone Wrong—Terror and Trafficking

Paradigms about the war on terror collide with trafficking to engender more challenging experiences for many migrants, especially migrants perceived to be Muslim, particularly if they are seeking work in the United States. Two men I interviewed, Amit and Sanjay (March 2012), both experienced the adverse effects of the war on terror discourse which helped place them in trafficking like situations. The influence of the war on terror paradigm pervades our notions of migrants and their racial and religious profiles; this conflation of migrants with Muslims, what sometimes follows as terrorists, created increased challenges for both men.

## Amit's Story

Amit was born and raised in Dubai to Indian parents who had migrated to the Gulf seeking employment. One of five children, Amit and his siblings grew up feeling "like second-class citizens in our own home" because strict citizenship contours prohibit migrants and their families from permanent immigration in the UAE and other parts of the Gulf. "Because of the politics in Dubai, we grew up with our parents always reminding us that we are guests here, that this isn't our home, so we must respect," recalled Amit. "But along with respect was fear. We knew we could get kicked out anytime, easily. We knew that we were second-class citizens because of the color of our skin, because we were Indian, this is something I grew up being aware of," he added. So, like many other young men with whom Amit attended high school, he decided to migrate to the United States to attend college. "I mean, my parents had told me, they had told me they left India to come to Dubai to make a better life for us, so we could achieve. So that's what I did. I worked hard and got into college in the U.S.!"

Unfortunately for Amit, however, two years after he arrived in North Carolina to attend college, 9/11 happened.

> Suddenly, everyone was looking at me funny. Before I knew it, I was a second-class citizen there too! Everyone asked me if I knew terrorists or had some in my family, it was very confusing because I told them I wasn't even Muslim.

Amit was able to remain in North Carolina to finish college, but after graduating he was met with a rude awakening. "Two weeks after graduation, I was still hanging around my college town and I was picked up by the police. They asked me what I was doing there, what my business was. I told them I had graduated and was looking for a job. But they wouldn't have it," Amit explained. After being arrested for loitering, he was held at a local police station. "They told me that I had to go back home immediately. They asked me where I was a citizen of, but that was tough. I told them I was an Indian citizen, but that wasn't my home. They didn't like that much."

Amit's story reinforces the notion that the war on terror paradigm and its negative castigation of Muslims and labeling of any foreigner resembling a Middle Eastern man as dangerous adversely affected how he was treated. He emphasized that had it not been for 9/11, he would have been able to remain in the United States, the country he then called home, and find work and settle. Prior to 9/11, his predecessors had more viable options of moving to the United States to build a new life. Unfortunately, after the war on trafficking paradigm, movement into the United States by minority groups from the Middle East and South Asia became increasingly restricted.

After a few weeks of detention, Amit was deported to India, a place that he had never called home. "It was very strange because I was sent to Bombay, and I mean, I had visited India a few times growing up, but I didn't remember it at all, and I had no family there, nothing. It's a very strange experience to be sent to a home you don't know," he reflected. Because he had been detained and deported, Amit had a difficult time acquiring a visa to enter the UAE to rejoin his family. After a year of living on the streets, living day-to-day, he was finally granted a tourist visa to visit his parents. He was contemplating illegally overstaying his visa and working at an underground bar in his parents' neighborhood in order to avoid deportation back to India, the home he didn't know.

### Sanjay's Story

For Sanjay, the paradigm of the war on terror directly affected his experience of trafficking. Two years after 9/11, Sanjay and his friends were trying to migrate to the United States having heard that there were many jobs for persons with experience working in oil refineries. "Many of us had been wanting to go to the U.S. to work, knowing we could get paid more, but we couldn't get visas after 9/11, so that was difficult," recalled Sanjay. Like many of his friends, Sanjay was struggling to make ends meet at home. Several local factories had been shut down due to challenges in the local economy, and for many people "migration meant survival," as one Indian construction worker in Dubai repeatedly told me.

One day Sanjay felt his luck had changed. "This guy John came to Gujarat (province in India) from the U.S. and told us about a new company. The job sounded really great. That guy said, he said he would help us get passports, visas, everything. He told us he would provide us with great living conditions, each of us getting our own room or house. It sounded like a great opportunity," Sanjay explained. Along with 29 other men from his neighborhood, Sanjay decided to pursue the offer. He recalled being amazed that John was able to procure visas for all 30 of the men without any of them even visiting the embassy. "It was amazing. We thought, this is a powerful man, and he will help us go places," he said.

When he arrived in Oklahoma, however, things were not as he had been promised. He was made to live with all of the other men in a small house without enough beds or facilities. "When we asked John, hey, wait, we need more than this, he just said 'I'm working on it'. But you know what he meant? He meant he was going to take five of the guys, who were supposed to come work on refining and building actual mechanical products, he took them to work on renovating this old warehouse, then we were moved in there when 20 other guys from India arrived. So, 50 of us living in that small warehouse," he explained. When they asked for pots and pans to cook with, or better running water, they were told to be happy with what they had. They were made to work long hours, often not engaging in the work that they thought they would be doing. "Yeah, so that guy John, that guy, he had us working as janitors, cooks, cleaners, and everything other than what we thought we would be doing." When one or more of the men fell ill, they were not permitted to go to the doctor. When a small group of the men asked to attend church at Christmas time, their request was denied.

"I remember it so well, he said, 'You do not go to church, you pray to me, I am your God, I provide everything you need.' And the same thing with going to the doctor, he said 'I am your doctor, I'll give you what medicines I think you need.' But that was not okay with us, we were upset, some of the guys started sneaking out," Sanjay explained. But when his boss received word that some of the men were sneaking out of the compound, he put locks on the warehouse door and compound gates and stationed armed guards at the fences.

> John came in and said, "No one is leaving. If you leave, the guards will kill you." But it was strange, and what was strange was his reason. He said to us "because of 9/11 and the war on terror, it is not safe for you to go out, that is why I'm putting on these locks, it's for your own good." He tried to scare us all the time about 9/11. He told us that if we did manage to escape, that the Americans around would kill us because they would assume we were terrorists. This worked for some of the guys who really were afraid to leave.

Sanjay explained that he and his friends deliberated ways to escape for many years. When they approached John collectively to ask for their visas and passports, John once again told them that he was keeping them "for their own good" (a phrase used by many traffickers, and even policies meant to restrict the movement of migrants). "What was funny though was that some of the guys kept sneaking out, and they managed to get to the church. When they got there, all the Americans were so nice, and it was them who ended up working with us to empower us to get out, they didn't hate us or want to kill us, it was just John," Sanjay recalled. After eight years of planning, finally one snowy night all of the men escaped by scaling the fence, jumping through the barbed wires, and running to the home of a local pastor. Fortunately a few of the men had met local residents at the church who assisted them in providing legal counsel. Less than a year after escaping, Sanjay had received a trafficking visa (as he had willingly testified against John, his trafficker) and was happily working in a town 30 miles from the one he had been trafficked to in Nebraska.

Both Amit and Sanjay were adversely affected by the racist undertones of war on terror paradigms. Terror and trafficking are conflated as interconnected processes, and because the discourse links them both to weak states, the Middle East, and Muslims, policies influenced by the war on terror in turn influence policies on the war on trafficking. The pressures of the war on terror paradigm to increase security, border controls, and policing (all with underlying racism) structure the contours of the situation similar to trafficking that both of these men and many others experienced. In this way, we see the trafficking and terror paradigms sutured to produce increasingly challenging situations for migrants. As delineated earlier in the chapter, structural change is needed to intervene, and it is imperative that paradigms about trafficking, terror, and traffickingandterror are revamped to recognize the realities of lived experience.

## Life After Trafficking

Within the saving rhetoric that is deeply embedded in the trafficking paradigm is a presumption that, once persons are saved or rescued, their lives will improve and that the war on trafficking will be rightly fought. The problem with this framing is twofold: (1) life after trafficking (whether back home in impoverished or war-torn countries, or living as an exile in a new country) can be worse than when persons were laboring under situations of force, fraud, or coercion, and (2) saving or rescue doesn't impact or readjust the structural conditions such as bad labor practices, weak labor laws, or poverty which can lead more persons to vulnerable situations. Two case studies from different parts of Asia and Africa illuminate just how challenging life *after* trafficking can be.

### *Yusil's Story*

Yusril is a fisherman from a small island off the coast of West Java, Indonesia. After hearing about work opportunities on a large fishing vessel near New Zealand, he was persuaded by two of his friends to pursue employment there. He had been working for many years in different parts of Indonesia, trying to make ends meet on small fishing boats to support his wife and daughters. After yet another small ship he worked on was destroyed, he decided to join his friend on the *Mariela*, a large fishing vessel operated by South Koreans, but docked off the coast of New Zealand. Upon arrival he was made to work 30–36 hour shifts, without sitting down, in the poorly lit, overcrowded underbelly of the ship. "We never saw daylight, everything was in darkness," he recalled. To make matters worse, he did not receive the level of compensation he was promised, and was sometimes abused by his employers when he or others agitated for better working conditions or higher wages.

In the spring of 2012, journalist and author Benjamin Skinner broke a story about Yusril and his friends (Skinner 2012). Skinner revealed that this vessel supplied the fish bought by large American corporations such as Costco, Walmart, and P.F. Chang's. Just before the story was released, Yusril and several of his friends had managed to stage an uprising and escape the terrible working conditions they were in. Once the story broke, others on the ship were freed as well. Unfortunately, the story does not end here. When Yusril and his friends managed to get off the *Mariela*, they were deported back to their local towns in Indonesia. Unable to find work there, Yusril is currently living hand to mouth, having constructed a small boat, which he uses to catch enough fish to feed his family. For Yusril, going home did not solve his problems, but rather amplified them; he is no longer able to get a job on a large fishing vessel because he has been blacklisted as an agitator. Given that he does not have skills or connections outside the fishing industry, he finds himself stuck without any labor mobility and unable to support his family.

## Makda's Story

Makda's story is similar. Born and raised in Eritrea, she decided to migrate to Dubai after her father was killed by guerillas who also kidnapped her mother. "There was nothing there for me back home but death and violence," Makda said, recalling the circumstances that impelled her to leave her home. Makda had a cousin who had moved to Dubai during the economic boom in 2006 who often wrote postcards and sent pictures of her life. She worked at a local hospital and told Makda that she could get work in Dubai easily once she came on a tourist visa. In 2008, Makda procured a tourist visa, borrowed money from friends with the promise that she would repay her debt, and made what she had hoped would be a permanent move to Dubai. "I thought, maybe life in Dubai will be hard, but at least I will be safe," she explained.

Unfortunately for Makda, however, she arrived in Dubai just as the economy was beginning to spiral downwards. There were no jobs available to her and her tourist visa expired quickly. Unable to make ends meet, she took an informal job at a karaoke bar in the Ethiopian neighborhood of Dubai given her linguistic strengths as an Amharic speaker. She worked at the bar for one year and was finally able to rent a room on her own after 10 months of sleeping on the floor of the small room her cousin shared with four other Eritrean women. "Things are starting to get better, I am liking Dubai, making friends. I finally feel safe," she told me in the summer of 2009.

One day I went back to the bar where I had met Makda, but the bar was boarded up. A local passerby told me that there had been a police raid on the bar because some people had rumored that it also operated as a brothel. Once I found a local policeman, he corroborated the story, explaining that the goal of the raid had been to "help the girls stuck inside." When I called Makda's cousin, she told me that Makda had been caught in the raid and that she was terrified her cousin had been deported. "If they send her back to Eritrea, she will either be killed because of her father, or starve to death," she told me. Several months later I called Makda's cousin again. "I just heard word from another cousin last week," she said. "Makda is nowhere to be found, no one knows what happened to her, but she has completely disappeared."

As "G" (whose epigraph begins the chapter) expertly reflected on the idea of rescue or getting out, the focus on rescuing one individual runs the risk of eclipsing the structural conditions which allow that kind of abuse to take place at all. Furthermore, we direct our attention away from both the challenges of life after trafficking, and the difficult decisions that migrants must make to enter situations where they may become vulnerable. In the next, final chapter, I reflect on some alternative ways of reading the wars on terror and trafficking, emphasizing specific recommendations at the discursive, policy, and activist levels that could be enacted to more closely align discourse, policy, and lived experience.

## DISCUSSION QUESTIONS

1. How can ethnographic research that reveals stories of lived experience (such as those presented in this chapter) help understand the contours of the wars on terror and trafficking?

2. How do these stories contradict the paradigms constructed about the experiences of those involved in illicit networks?

3. How can we extrapolate from ethnography so that the stories of a few can illuminate the challenges experienced by many? How do we look at individual stories to understand structural problems?

# V: Conclusion:
## Towards a New Paradigm

The "wars" of today, like the war on drugs, war on terror or even war on trafficking, they are actually wars on humanity, not wars on a problem. When you declare these types of wars there will always be violence, and the most vulnerable will always suffer. Maybe governments should consider declaring peace on these issues, not war.

(interview with Juan "Sebastian" Escobar, July 2012)

A few weeks before completing this book, I had the opportunity to interview Juan "Sebastian" Escobar, son of the famed Colombian drug dealer, Pablo Escobar. The conversation was framed around the question of intersecting areas of the informal economy. He discussed his opinions on underground economies, informal economies, and illicit networks. While Sebastian noted that drug trafficking and arms smuggling did have some links, he was emphatic that other types of illicit networks such as human trafficking, terrorism, or organ brokering did not necessarily overlap, except insofar as they incite the same type of moral panic. "In Latin America, our burden has been the war on drugs. Because of the U.S. and the 'war on drugs,' people think Latin America, they think drugs. The problem is that this war has cost more people their lives than it has helped anyone," he reflected. When I described the traffickingandterror paradigm that I had been writing about he nodded in agreement. "Yes, that is the burden of the Middle East, and of Muslims. War on terror and war on trafficking, I see how they have done that, but it's just breeding more violence isn't it?" he asked rhetorically.

The approach to solving challenges presented by trafficking, drugs, or terrorism has yielded an aggressive response on the part of U.S. policy makers. Declaring war on the issues does suggest a strong commitment to tackling the challenges, but as my conversation with Sebastian Escobar illuminates, the wars have incited violence, whether structural, systemic, or physical. Moreover, and perhaps just as important, when governments declare these wars (on terror, trafficking, drugs, or a combination), racial and ethnic undertones persist. As Escobar noted, the war on drugs was very much framed as a war against an unknown enemy, but one who was thought to be housed in Latin America. As he, and many other scholars of the war on drugs noted, the underlying rhetoric was directed against constructing a negative image of many

Latin Americans who suffered during this period. Similarly, both the wars on terror and trafficking rely on inciting moral panic aimed at Muslim and Middle Eastern populations, collapsed into one monolithic category of "terrifying Muslims" (Rana 2011). Instead of considering the structural violence that frames challenges for those most adversely affected by terror, trafficking, or drugs, the government declaration of a war on X, has the opposite effect of further marginalizing already marginalized populations. Those most in need of recognition, agency, assistance, find themselves further challenged not only by the various types of violence they are up against, but a new form of discursive violence that paints them all as victims in need of saving or villains in need of prosecution.

As much of this book has shown, the rhetoric that falls from the traffickingandterror paradigm leads to policies, discourses, and responses that (1) paint all Muslims and Middle Easterners as "terrifying Muslims" (Rana 2011); (2) portray women, particularly women in the Middle East, or those interacting with "terrifying Muslim men" as without agency and in desperate need of saving; and (3) can be used as anti-immigration means and sentiments. Kneejerk saving and rescue responses typically have the opposite of their intended effect. Beyond rescue campaigns being unproductive and sometimes harming populations, is the reality that a focus on saving or rescue eclipses the larger structural issues such as poverty, wars, violence and government complicity in legal productions of illegality. Furthermore, a closer look at lived realities of those living through and most adversely affected by the wars on terror and trafficking reveals that individuals are challenged not by the act of terror or trafficking, but by the discourses of terror, trafficking, and the fused paradigm of traffickingandterror.

A decade into the most recent war on terror and war on trafficking, the linkages between these two socially constructed wars becomes both clearer and more opaque at the same time. What is more opaque are the interconnections presupposed by rhetoric that assumes that persons involved in trafficking are also involved in terrorism and vice versa. Despite numerous studies, this connection remains without verification or data, and those insisting on the fusion acknowledge the conjectural nature of their arguments. What can be seen more clearly, however, are the similarities in responses and constructed discourse about both trafficking and terror and the deployment (or result) of moral panic as a lens through which to talk about traffickingandterror as a single fused concept within a paradigm of panic over security of borders, purity of populations, and the economic world order. The socially constructed nature of the discursive underpinnings of these wars is important in highlighting the need to challenge the paradigm, resist the reification or demonization of populations, and rethink approaches to the large-scale challenges these discourses have led to such as immigration reform, deportation regimes, and large-scale economic reforms such as structural adjustment policies. Why the wars on terror and trafficking have been not only produced but have also reinforced one another must also be questioned in order to understand our racialized, sociopolitical moment which some might call a response to a "clash of civilizations" (Huntington 1996).

It is true that the wars on terror and trafficking are linked, although not in the way the traffickingandterror paradigm would presume. Rather, their linkages come in the fact that they are both discursive productions taking the form of moral crusades constructed at a political moment to serve the interests of some while violating the rights of many. Trafficking and terror are connected in the similarities of the responses to the two which include increased policing, criminalization, tightening of borders, and the focus on keeping particular populations "in" and others "out." They are similar and linked in that individuals are blamed or castigated as a threat which obscures the larger macro-social issues and ignores difficult questions such as: who are the individuals deemed as threats? Why do they occupy the spaces they do? What is the level of government complicity in producing or relying on shadow economies? Why do individuals need to leave their homes to make ends meet?

The linkages described above take the form of similarities and produce a series of erroneous connections which eclipse the similarities in the adverse effects of not only the wars on terror and trafficking, but the fallout from the traffickingandterror paradigm. The paradigm which fuses trafficking and terror, both rests on and reproduces Islamophobic rhetoric bolstering calls for increased surveillance of Muslim populations both abroad and in the United States. A portrait from the traffickingandterror paradigm of Muslim men as terrorists, nefarious smugglers, and members of threatening illicit networks has emerged. These are men who need to be monitored and contained as much for their voracious sexual appetites as for their capacity to undermine security and world order. By contrast, women in Muslim countries are seen as either victims of these men or of their own circumstances, susceptible to kidnapping, trafficking, and the possibility of falling prey to the draw of illicit networks. These women, the paradigm suggests, need to be saved; how that saving is to occur remains opaque.

The traffickingandterror paradigm reproduces a racialized morality that adversely effects migrants, Muslims, and anyone castigated as an "other." It is the discourse, and not the threat of these illicit networks per se, that is threatening already vulnerable populations. But it does not have to be this way. It is possible to shift the problematic responses to these issues simply by shifting our paradigms about what trafficking is and is not, what terrorism entails and does not entail, who is involved in these areas of illicit networks (and indeed what we even mean by the term "illicit networks" and how loaded this term is), what the structural conditions and factors are, and the level of complicity of formal or legal institutions and bodies. Policy and discourse can be reformed to reflect more accurately the realities of those most affected by the challenges of both trafficking and terror. Discourses heavily impact lived experience, and by changing our paradigms, we can have more honest conversations that seek to hold corporations, governments, and even ourselves accountable. We can push for better and stronger policies. And the good news is that with technology we can harness the power of technology to not only get the message out, but to empower migrants and leverage change. By bringing policies in line with lived experience and by declaring peace, not war, on issues and committing to rights-based solutions rather than further militarization, we can hope to create a more robust conversation to understand the actual problems so we can come up with actual solutions and move beyond the racialized and gendered stereotypes implied in the traffickingandterror paradigm.

## DISCUSSION QUESTIONS

1. What have been the long-term consequences of the socially constructed wars on terror and trafficking?
2. What types of policies can better serve the needs of populations marginalized by the traffickingandterror paradigm?
3. How can we shatter the traffickingandterror paradigm and expose its weaknesses and falsities?

# Bibiliography

The 700 Club. n.d. Ashley Judd interview. Retrieved from (http://www.cbn.com/700club/guests/bios/ashley_judd041111.aspx).

Abu Lughod, Lila. 2002. "Do Muslim women really need saving? Anthropological reflections on cultural relativism and its others." *American Anthropologists 104*(3): 783–90.

Andreas, P. 2011. "Illicit Globalization: Myths, Misconceptions, and Historical Lessons." *Political Science Quarterly 126*(3): 403–25.

Atty, I., and W. VonSchendel, eds. 2005. *Illicit Flows and Criminal Things: States, Borders and the Other Side of Globalization.* Bloomington: Indiana University Press.

Bavelaar, Rhama. 2005. "'Moral Panic' and the Muslim." Retrieved June 3, 2009 from IslamOnline.

Bernstein, E. 2007. *Temporarily Yours: Intimacy, Authenticity and the Commerce of Sex.* Chicago: University of Chicago Press.

Bernstein, E., and L. Schaffner, eds. 2005. *Regulating Sex: The Politics of Intimacy and Identity.* New York: Routledge.

*Blood Diamond.* 2006. DVD. Directed by Edward Zwick; written by Charles Leavitt and C. Gaby Mitchell. USA and Germany: Warner Brothers.

Bourgois, Philippe. 1996. *In Search of Respect: Selling Crack in El Barrio.* Cambridge: Cambridge University Press.

Bourne, M. 2011. "Netwar Geopolitics: Security, Failed States and Illicit Flows." *The British Journal of Politics and International Relations 13*(4): 490–513.

California General Election Official Voter Information Guide. (2012. Prop 35. Human trafficking. Penalties. Initiative statute. Retrieved from (http://voterguide.sos.ca.gov/propositions/35).

*Call and Response.* 2008. DVD. Directed by Justin Dillon; written by Justin Dillon and Shadd Williams. USA: Fair Trade Pictures

Castells, Manuel. 1999. *Information Technology, Globalization and Social Development.* Geneva: United Nations Research Institute.

Cheng, Sealing. 2010. *On the Move for Love: Migrant Entertainers and the U.S. Military in South Korea.* Philadelphia: University of Pennsylvania Press.

Cohen, Debra. 2011. *Braceros: Migrant Citizens and Transnational Subjects in the Postwar United States and Mexico.* Chapel Hill: University of North Carolina Press.

Cohen, Stanley. 1972. *Folk Devils and Moral Panics: The Creation of the Mods and Rockers.* London: MacGibbon and Kee.

Constable, Nicole. 2010. *Migrant Workers in Asia: Distant Divides, Intimate Connections.* London: Routledge.

De Genova, N. 2004. "The Legal Production of Mexican/Migrant 'llegality.'" *Latino Studies 2:* 160–85.

De Genova, N., and N. Peutz. 2010. *The Deportation Regime: Sovereignty, Space and the Freedom of Movement.* Durham, NC: Duke University Press.

Doezema, Jo. 2005. "Now You See Her, Now You Don't: Sex Workers at the UN Trafficking Protocol Negotiation." *Social Legal Studies 14*(1), 61–89.

Duneier, Mitchell. 1999. *Sidewalk.* New York: Farrar, Straus and Giroux.

Foucault, Michel. 1972. *The Archaeology of Knowledge.* London: Routledge.

Garcés Mascareñas, Blanca. 2010. "Legal Production of Illegality from a Comparative Perspective: The Cases of Malaysia and Spain." *Asia Europe Journal 8*(1), 77–89.

Gardner, A. 2010. *City of Strangers: Gulf Migration and the Indian Community in Bahrain.* Ithaca, NY: Cornell Press.

Goode, E., and N. Ben-Yehuda. 1994. *Moral Panics: The Social Construction of Deviance.* New York: Wiley Blackwell.

Holt, V. K., and A. J. Boucher. 2009. "Framing the Issue: UN Responses to Corruption and Criminal Networks in Post-Conflict Settings." *International Peacekeeping 16*(1): 20–32.

Hopper, Kim. 2002. *Reckoning with Homelessness.* Itaca, NY: Cornell University Press.

Howard, Russel D., and Colleen M. Traughber. 2007. "The Routes of Trafficking from Central Asia to Western Europe." *Connections: The Quarterly Journal VI*(1): 1–5.

*Human Trafficking.* 2005. TV Movie/DVD. Directed by Christian Duguay; written by Carole Doyle and Agatha Dominik. Canada and USA: For Sale Productions.

Huntington, Samuel. 1996. *Clash of Civilizationsand the Remaking of World Order.* New York: Simon and Schuster.

*Hustle and Flow.* 2005. DVD. Written and directed by Craig Brewer. USA: Crunk Pictures.

*International Narcotics Control Strategy Report.* n.d. http://www.state.gov/j/inl/rls/nrcrpt/2012/

Jordan, Ann.2012.Remarks at Google Ideas roundtable "Rescue Reconsidered."

Koyama. 2011. Retrieved from (http://eminism.org/blog/entry/231).

Longva, A. N. 1999. "Keeping Migrant Workers in Check: The Kafala System in the Gulf." *Middle East Report* 211: 20–22.

Longva, A. N. 2005. "Neither Autocracy Nor Democracy But Ethnocracy: Citizens, Expatriates, and the Socio-Political Regime in Kuwait." Pp. 114–35 in *Monarchies and Nations — Globalisation and Identity in the Arab States of the Gulf,* ed. Paul Dresch and James Piscatori. London: I.B. Tauris.

Mahdavi, Pardis. 2011. *Gridlock: Labor, Migration and Human Trafficking in Dubai.* Palo Alto, CA: Stanford University Press.

Mahmood, Saba. 2004. *Politics of Piety: The Islamic Revival and the Feminist Subject.* Princeton, NJ: Princeton University Press.

Malm, A. E., J. B. Kinney, and N. R. Pollard. (2008). Social Network and Distance Correlates of Criminal Associates Involved in Illicit Drug Production. *Security Journal, 21*(1–2): 77–94.

Mamdani, Mahmood. 2001. *When Victims Become Killers: Colonialism, Nativism, and the Genocide in Rwanda*. Princeton, NJ: Princeton University Press.

*Mammoth.* 2009. DVD. Directed by Lukas Moodysson, screenplay by Lukas Moodysson. Stockholm, Sweden: Memfis Film.

Marx, Karl and Fredrick Engels. 1848/1969. Manifesto of the Communist Party. Pp. 98–137 in *Selected Works volume 1*. Moscow: Progress Publishers.

Massad, Joseph. 2008. *Desiring Arabs*. Chicago: University of Chicago Press.

Mitchell, Don. 2011 (April 12). Lecture given at the Huntington Libraries, Los Angeles, California.

Naím, Moisés. 2012. "The Rise of the Mafia State." *Foreign Affairs* (April 25).

O'Connell Davidson, J. 2006. "Will the Real Sex Slave Please Stand Up?" *Feminist Review 83*: 4–22.

Parreñas, R. S. 2011. *Illicit Flirtations: Labor, Migration and Sex Trafficking in Tokyo*. Stanford, CA: Stanford University Press.

Philippines Household Reform Act of 2006. Retrieved from (http://centerformigrantadvocacy.files. wordpress.com/2012/06/household-service-workers-policy-reform-package.pdf).

Puar, Jasbir K. 2004. "Abu Ghraib: Arguing against Exceptionalism." *Feminist Studies 30*(2): 522–34.

Puar, Jasbir. 2007. *Terrorist Assemblages*. Durham, NC: Duke University Press.

Puar, Jasbir K., and Amit Rai. 2002. "Monster, Terrorist, Fag: The War on Terrorism and the Production of Docile Patriots." *Social Text 20*(3): 117–48.

Rana, Junaid. 2011. *Terrifying Muslims: Race, Labor and the South Asian Diaspora*. Durham, NC: Duke University Press.

*The Report to the Division for the Advancement of Women from the Best Practices Policy Project*. 2005. Retrieved from (http://www.un.org/womenwatch/daw/vaw/ngocontribute/BEST%20PRAC-TICES%20POLICY%20PROJECT.pdf).

Rothe, D. L., & Collins, V. 2011. An Exploration of Applying System Criminality to Arms Trafficking. *International Criminal Justice Review 21*(1): 22–28.

Said, Edward. 1978. *Orientalism*. New York: Pantheon Books.

Sajoo, A. B., ed. 2004. *Civil Society in the Muslim World: Contemporary Perspectives*. London: I.B. Tauris Press.

Siskin, Liana Sun and Alison Wyler. 2010. "Trafficking in Persons: U.S. Policy and Issues for Congress." Retrieved September 12, 2012 from (http://fpc.state.gov/documents/organization/139278.pdf).

Skinner, E. Benjamin. 2012 (March 30). "Slaves Put Squid on Dining Tables from South Pacific." Bloomberg. Retrieved from (http://www.bloomberg.com/news/2012-02-23/slaves-put-squid-on-u-s-diningtables-from-south-pacific-catch.html).

Spivak, Gayatri. 2006. *In Other Worlds: Essays in Cultural Politics*. New York: Routledge.

Stop Child Sex Trafficking Now (SCTNow). n.d. Retrieved from (http:// www.sctnow.org).

*Taken.* 2009. DVD. Directed by Pierre Morel; written by Luc Besson and Robert Mark Kamen. USA: EuropaCorp.

Trafficking in Wrongs: Why Californians Need To Vote No on Prop 35 and Why the Rest of Us Should Care. n.d. Retrieved from (http://jezebel.com/5957894/trafficking-in-wrongs-why-californians-need-to-vote-no-on-prop-35-and-why-the-rest-of-us-should-care).

United Nations Palermo Protocol. 2000. Retieved from (http://www.palermoprotocol.com).

*U.S. Trafficking in Persons Report* (TIP). n.d. http://www.state.gov/j/tip/rls/tiprpt/

U.S. Trafficking Victims Protection Act (TVPA). n.d. Retrieved from (http://www.state.gov/documents/organization/10492.pdf).

Vance, C. S. 2011. "States of Contradiction: Twelve Ways to Do Nothing about Trafficking While Pretending To." *Social Research 7* (3): 933–48.

Vance, Carole, and A. M. Miller. 2004. *Sexuality, Human Rights, and Health. Health and Human Rights 7* (2): 5–15.

Walkowitz, Judith. 1992. *City of Dreadful Delight: Narratives of Sexual Danger in Late Victorian London.* Chicago: University of Chicago Press.

Weitzer, Ronald. 2007. "The Social Construction of Sex Trafficking: Ideology and Institutionalization of a Moral Crusade." *Politics & Society; Affilia* (May 1): 142–52.

Wijers, Marianne. 1998. Women, Labor and Migration: The Position of Trafficked Women and Strategies for Support. Pp. 69–79 in *Global Sex Workers: Rights, Resistance and Redefinition*, eds. K. Kempadoo and J. Doezema. New York: Routledge.

Williams, Phil and Vanda Felbab Brown. 2012. "Drug Trafficking, Violence and Instability". *Strategic Studies Initiative,* 1–88.

# Glossary/Index

~~~~~~

9/11 20, 26, 39, 42 57, 67–69 (*see also* September 11, 2001)

**A**

Abu Lughod, Lila 17, 36, 41

**agency:**    the ability to act as an individual and to determine one's own fate 4, 12, 13, 16, 17, 23, 36, 41, 58, 61, 63, 74

Agricultural worker 3, 8, 35, 44, 45, 57 (*see also* Bracero guest worker)

    limited rights and documentation status 45

    survivor of labor trafficking 35

American Civil Liberties Union 2

Atty, I. 41

**B**

Ben-Yehuda, N. 4, 7

Bernstein, E, 20, 25, 31, 61

*Blood Diamond* 35

**Bracero guest worker:**    The Bracero program was a guest worker program initiated in the United States in 1942. The term Bracero comes from the Spanish "strong arm," and the program structured the contours of the temporary migrant labor program for laborers who were brought from Mexico to the United States to meet growing demand for cheap labor during World War II. 45

Boucher, A. J. 46

Bourgois, Philippe 49

Bourne, M. 44, 47, 48, 51, 52, 53, 54

Brown, Vanda Felbab 54

Bush, George W. 16, 19, 63

**C**

California General Election Official Voter Information Guide 1, 2–4, 29, 45

Californians Against Sexual Exploitation Act (CASE)/Proposition 35 1–8, 11, 29$n$6

Marx, Karl 32

Massad, Joseph 26, 27

Microsoft 18, 37–38

Migration 7–8, 13, 15–17, 31, 39, 46, 66

    Bracero Act 45

    City of Hope 65

    single men 17, 68–69

    single women 17, 22, 62–64, 71

Miller, A. M. 7

Mitchell, Don 32, 45

**moral panic:**   According to Stanley Cohen, author of *Folk Devils and Moral Panics* (1972), a moral panic occurs when "[a] condition, episode, person or group of persons emerges to become defined as a threat to societal values and interests" (2). The language of moral panic typically harnesses a sense of moral indignation to create a category of villains or "folk devils" which the public is to rally against. 1, 4

    reefer madness 6

    crack moms and babies 6

    U.S. war on drugs 6

    Red Scare 6

    white slave trade 7–8, 11*n*1, 28, 29*n*6

**moral crusade:**   a large-scale moral panic wherein the claims about particular issues and the way they are framed are often infused with a sense of morality and are more damaging than the actual conditions 4–9, 11, 27, 73

Musahib, Sharla 29

Muslims, fear of 8–9, 10, 15–17, 25–27, 42, 74


**N**

Naím, Moisés 30

Nicole, Jessie 50


**O**

O'Connell Davidson, J. 16

organized crime 14–15, 22, 24, 27, 30, 33–34, 39, 44–45

"othering" 7, 11, 20, 25–27, 44, 58, 75


**P**

**Palermo Protocol:**   Colloquial name for the United Nations Protocol to Prevent, Suppress and Punish Trafficking in Persons, Especially Women and Children. The protocol was compiled and passed in Palermo, Italy, in 2000 and is considered one of the largest wide-scale responses to human trafficking today. 2, 15, 21, 29, 52, 63

Parreñas, R. S. 64

Peutz. N. 61

**Philippine Household Service Reform Package:** an act passed in the Philippines in 2006 for the purpose of securing more rights and protections for Filipinos migrating across borders into the domestic work industry 50

Pollard, N. R. 52

Proposition 35/Californians Against Sexual Exploitation Act (CASE) 1–8, 11, 29n6

Puar, Jasbir K., 17, 26, 27


**R**

**racialized morality:** Moralizing rhetoric that locates particular racial or ethnic groups as sources of moral failings. This form of morality inadvertently reinforces distinctions between white saviors and the minorities who require their help and interference. 4, 7, 58, 75

Rai, Amit 26, 27

Rana, Junaid 16, 17, 51, 79

rescue campaigns 3, 17–18, 29, 57, 58–62

Rothe, D. L. 49, 52


**S**

Said, Edward 26

Sajoo, A. B. 29

September 11, 2001 11; (*see also* 9/11)

**sex trafficking:** the movement of persons by force, fraud, or coercion into the sex industry 2, 16, 19, 31, 54

**sex work:** According to the United Nations Division for the Advancement of Women, the term "sex work" or "commercial sex work" is generally understood to involve a wide range of behaviors and venues, and includes, but is not limited to, street prostitution, brothel prostitution, exotic dancing, paid domination, and sexual massage. Many people who engage in sex work or commercial sex identify what they do as sex work, but it is also important to acknowledge that many other people who engage in informal and occasional sexual transactions may not incorporate this experience as an important part of their personal identity. 4, 11, 42, 60

Shih, Elena 60

Silicon Valley 25, 37–39

Siskin, Liana Sun 53, 54, 55

Skinner, Ben 32–33, 39, 70

**social construction:**  The social constructionist perspective highlights the fact that "social conditions become 'problems' only as a result of claims-making by interested parties, claims that may or may not reflect actual social arrangements" (Weitzer 2007: 448). In other words, that panics are socially constructed highlights the fact that the problems are not natural or existing problems, but are created by a group or multiple groups with particular agendas. This construction comes in the form of crafting narratives or messaging campaigns. 42

**structural violence:**  Inequalities perpetuated by systems, structures, states, or other sources of power, often based on race, class, and gender. These systemic inequalities harm and disadvantage individuals, resulting in physical and emotional challenges. 32, 55, 58, 74

**surveillance:**  A politicized form of observation that usually entails monitoring certain individuals or populations with an agenda. Sometimes this observation can be positive, but it is often negative as it shows exertions of power by the observer on the observed. 8, 16, 26, 37, 64, 75

**surveillance of sexuality:**  observation or monitoring of the intimate lives, erotic fantasies, or portrayals of sexuality pertaining to certain populations 12

# T

**trafficking:**  The official definition of trafficking as stated in Article 3, paragraph (a) of the Protocol to Prevent, Suppress and Punish Trafficking in Persons prepared by the United Nations Office of Drug Control is as follows: "the recruitment, transportation, transfer, harbouring or receipt of persons, by means of the threat or use of force or other forms of coercion, of abduction, of fraud, of deception, of the abuse of power or of a position of vulnerability or of the giving or receiving of payments or benefits to achieve the consent of a person having control over another person, for the purpose of exploitation. Exploitation shall include, at a minimum, the exploitation of the prostitution of others or other forms of sexual exploitation, forced labour or services, slavery or practices similar to slavery, servitude or the removal of organs." 1, 10, 24, 41, 57, 73

**Trafficking in Persons Report (TIP):**  a global scorecard compiled by the United
  States Office to Monitor and Combat Trafficking in Persons which is released
  every year and ranks countries around the world into one of four tiers depending
  on perceived responses to human trafficking within a particular nation's borders.
  10, 11, 29, 47
  Islamophobia 16
  Iran 10
  Musahib, Sharla 29
Trafficking in Wrongs: Why Californians Need To Vote No on Prop 35 and Why
  the Rest of Us Should Care 3
Traughber, Colleen M. 30, 41
**tropes:**  stereotypes, paradigms, or metaphors that are often overused to the point
  of becoming clichés 18, 23, 63

# U
United Nations 47, 55, 63
  definition of sex work 13, 63
  Office of Drug Control 14–15, 29
  Palermo Protocol 2, 21
  Peace operations 46
U.S. foreign policy 11, 30, 41
U.S. Trafficking in Persons Report (TIP) 10–11
U.S. Trafficking Victims Protection Act (TVPA) 13, 21, 27, 29, 47, 63

# V
Vance, C. S. 7, 20, 46, 47, 48, 53, 54
VonSchendel, W. 41

# W
Walkowitz, Judith 7
Wall Street 25, 31–33
**War on trafficking:**  A discursive turn of phrase articulated during the George W.
  Bush presidency referring to a commitment on the part of the U.S. government
  to combat and prevent human trafficking. This metaphoric war, like the war
  on drugs, does not have a clear beginning or ending point, and governmental
  strategies to end trafficking remain opaque. The contours of the war on trafficking are perhaps best exemplified in a close reading of the United States' domestic
  and international policies on trafficking such as the Trafficking Victims Protection Act and the Trafficking in Persons Report as they have played a major role
  in structuring the discourse on trafficking, and can also be read as products of

discourse and debates about trafficking, migration, and sex work. 1, 10, 18, 42, 58, 83.

**war on terror:**   A phrase first used by President George W. Bush to denote a military, legal, and ideological struggle against regimes and organizations that were labeled as "terrorists." More conceptually, the war on terror is about separating good Muslims from bad Muslims (Mamdani 2001) and producing a category of terrifying Muslims (Rana 2011) requiring intense surveillance at best and more often harsh responses such as intervention and detention. Used to justify intervention and military occupation of countries such as Afghanistan and Iraq, the term has also become emblematic of a witch hunt of sorts wherein it is not clear when or how this war could or would be won, and when or how it would end. 1, 5, 11, 42, 58, 73

# Custom Materials
## DELIVER A MORE REWARDING EDUCATIONAL EXPERIENCE.

## The Social Issues Collection

This unique collection features 250 readings plus 45 recently added readings for undergraduate teaching in sociology and other social science courses. The social issues collection includes selections from Joe Nevins, Sheldon Elkand-Olson, Val Jenness, Sarah Fenstermaker, Nikki Jones, France Winddance Twine, Scott McNall, Ananya Roy, Joel Best, Michael Apple, and more.

**1** Go to the website at
routledge.customgateway.com

**2** Choose from almost 300
readings from Routledge
& other publishers

**3** Create your complete
custom anthology

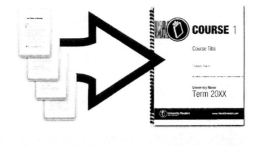

COURSE 1

Course Title

University Name
Term 20XX